THE BEGINNER'S GUIDE

CULTIVATING SUCCESS IN
INDIVIDUALS, TEAMS & BUSINESSES

CAROLINE BEARDALL

First published 2023

ISBN: 978-1-916844-01-8

Published by The HEAD Gardener

Design and print management by Verité CM Ltd,
Worthing BN12 4HF
+44 (0) 1903 241975

THE BEGINNER'S GUIDE

CULTIVATING SUCCESS IN
INDIVIDUALS, TEAMS & BUSINESSES

ACKNOWLEDGEMENTS

Bunny, it is your love that makes this possible.

Thank you to my friends and family – just by being who you are you have helped create this.

For my professional colleagues, the best of you and worst of you have all made my garden grow, so I can help others.

And with eternal wonder and praise to Him, without whom none of this would be.

CONTENTS

PART 1

PART 2

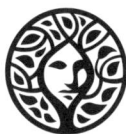

PART 3

PROLOGUE

The great thing about a garden is that you can look, see and experience it your own way in your own time and take away ideas or memories that are just yours. So it is with HEAD gardening. We all have one, a head that is, and if you think about it, we all experience life differently, even when it's the same moment, job, company or anything we see hear feel touch or smell. Yet, we are made up of so many similarities and structures that we can adapt and flex – or not – to the prevailing conditions and circumstances.

So saying, that I realised that if you think of a garden, any garden, your vision will be different to mine, even if we are thinking about the same garden! And that is what is brilliant about HEAD Gardening, your garden is unique as an individual, you can create combined gardens in teams or grow businesses which succeed.

As with a garden you can go where you like, start where you like and create – or in the language of The HEAD Gardener 'cultivate'

– success for yourself, your teams, your organisation, even your family and friends.

Gardeners are optimists by nature – they have to be with so many untamed changes in our climate. I believe that those who lead others, and those who have ambition to lead and carve the path to success, also know that resetting, hard work and positivity are fundamental pre-requisites for success. I know it can be hard and I know sometimes that success can evade us, but with a bit of support we are the creatures who can survive pretty much anything if we have to, and still grow!

Finally, I wrote this book because I want to help you, your business and the way work works, to be truly better than it is. There is much said on leadership and management, many models and great 'gurus' to turn to, but I want to give you something that wherever you are in the world, whatever business or corner of the planet you inhabit you can look at a garden (big, small, roof, lush, scrub, public, private and prized) and connect your growth with the way nature intended you to be, strong, vibrant, happy and productive. What else are we here for?

PART 1

Introduction

The Model and Method

INTRODUCTION

People are like gardens.

Growing people to perform at their best is the same as achieving a productive, beautiful or new garden. It's not farming because in that agricultural industry there the cycle of planting and harvesting is continuous. Gardening is more evolutionary, in every sense, and you don't really need to know anything about it to start off! It does take effort, a plan (big or small) and a few good tools and techniques to cultivate the success you are looking for. And that's where I come in, I am the HEAD Gardener. To be a gardener at all you have to be an optimist and believe in tomorrow – and I do, quick fixes are short lived.

So let's get started!

For the impatient amongst you, is this something you need? What will it give you? How does it work? And what's so different about this than any other coaching or consulting model? You will want to see the model NOW, have a 'just give it to me and I will work it out' approach, and honestly, yes, yes you can do that! You can have a quick scan, get the idea and have a go, you really can. Like kids gardening, they want a quick return on their effort and so we tend to start them with something easy to plant (or in our professional language a quick sale and easy to win). We plant something small but a quickly gratifying product, be that flowers or edibles. You don't need any skill. But then these trainee humans begin to want something bigger or better from their garden – maybe the designers amongst them will want to change the way it is set up, or the hungry or greedy will want more, different, bigger produce… or they lose interest and say 'is that it?'. Do you know any people or businesses like that?

As well as for my impatient reader, this book is mainly for those who truly want to cultivate long term, enduring success, to leave a legacy of their own individual or businesses impact on the world. These are people who have looked in awe on visits to open gardens, or National Trust, RHS Chelsea (other garden displays are available!) where they stop you in your tracks at the beauty, the fragrance, the structure and the experience of living.

These readers might also be people who actually know how to garden, and have regular fights with their own small plot or grand acres, and who know that it takes time, hard graft and consistent care to journey to a mature garden. Although no gardening knowledge is required in this model, for these gardeners it will be the translation of that which they already know, and do literally, to do it in their heads, share in their teams and grow their organisations more organically or deliberately than ever before. That takes skill and thought.

TOP TIP

To garden you have to know what you are planting where, when it will 'come to life', how to help it with the right additional mulch or fertiliser (organic or otherwise) and then you will need to keep the pests away from the juicy shoots and that can include overindulgence in things they need, such as sun or water.

To 'HEAD' garden, you need the same, and be prepared to work for it. This is not some soft fluffy idea of smelling the roses and all saying how marvellous we are. This is about getting your hands dirty and making yourself and those around you grow!! Working out what you are trying to achieve, in what order, dealing with obstacles and competitors along the way, and not indulging in too much self-congratulatory activities, even though reward is important.

Take any chapter if you wish and start wherever your interest is piqued or where your need is greatest. The book is structured in a way which will outline the model in Part 1, then in Part 2 we move to considering some of the basic HEAD gardening tools and techniques that you will likely need whatever state your head garden is now or wants to be. Then in Part 3 I provide some thought leadership and stimulus for your own ideas by exploring 4 key topics of cultivating success in the world we live in.

We will also take a wander together through thoughts and ideas, come up with checklists or vision plans which you can choose to implement or simply notice and come back to. That's the thing with a garden, it doesn't appear or disappear without some signals that it's coming or going. That's true of people too, but we are often too busy or distracted to notice them 'quietly quit' or burnout until it's too late.

And as the seasons come and go and the sun rises on every garden, every day, so must it set, and so I do also explore mature gardens (individual heads and companies), the overgrown garden and those gently receding back to nature. So it is with ourselves in our careers and businesses. We, they, have a lifecycle. Sometimes longer sometimes shorter than we expect and had planned for, but there also some surprising discoveries and revivals that are possible too in ourselves as well as the lives we want to lead. Remember Tim Smit and The Lost Gardens of Heligan? Perhaps there is a garden within all of our heads that could bring joy and renewal to ourselves and those around us if we went and had a look?

In essence nature will do what it likes – like people – but with some nurture and focus amazing things can happen too!

Exercise 1

(You can do this in your teams or just as an individual)

Bring to mind a garden that you know well. It might be your own, a friend's, a public park garden or a managed garden by some big estate.

What do you notice about it?

What does it look, smell, sound, feel like to be there?

What do you like about it?

What don't you like about it?

Now imagine yourself as a garden, what sort of garden are you? A formal flower garden? A rose garden? Productive vegetable garden? Grand walled garden? A small, terraced house garden? Any sort of garden will do whatever comes to mind.

Jot a few notes of key features.

We start with this exercise to begin to get inside the model of the HEAD Gardener and to begin to understand the language we will be using and what it means to you to take a walk around your own head as a garden, or your organisation as a garden.

Maybe you described one with great ambition and a clear vision but not the skill to make it so. Maybe it is one which is well kept, doesn't cause comment, is tidy and pleasant to look at – is that your working life? If we look at the garden we can see both actual delivery (what's growing) potential (green shoots) or even nothing yet but a known planting plan for future achievements. Then there are those plants (attributes) that no longer serve you, in your own self, team or organisation that have 'gone over' and need either dead heading or pulling out, drying and replanting next year.

There are those you no longer want where they are, so need to be dug out. Some to plant elsewhere, some to put on the compost heap. Don't forget, even bad experiences, weeds and 'gone to seed' plants and people can be used to learn from – in the case of plants they rot down and then are used for their nutrients to help others grow later on. For people, it's the learning from those whose behaviour is not acceptable or who hurt others by their own actions that we can dig out and use as examples to make sure we don't perpetuate that.

Before we dive into the model, let's have a look at the sorts of context where HEAD Gardenening works, so that you can see how it applies to you both as a person and within your environment. The HEAD Gardener focusses on three main services using the model, from Coach, Consultant, and Facilitator.

Success is cultivated by meeting and exceeding potential – because growth adds value and needs both nourishment and deliberate focus to do so!

The specific services for this approach are:

Consulting

- Strategy / developing vision (hard landscaping)
- Achieving clarity for action (priority gardening)
- Undertaking change (from preparing the ground to reviving overgrown gardens and setting the new structure and planting plan)
- Analysing Team Development needs and creating their growth plan

Coaching

- (Re)Building hope, trust and teams (watering, sunshine, improving the 'soil')
- Navigation and positioning in teams (which 'plants' like what conditions)
- The 'productive' garden – getting more!
- Challenging the status quo – no more 'same old same old'
- Changing me and changing you – from caterpillar to butterfly
- Transition Coach – for individuals and their new organisation

Facilitation

- Action Learning for Teams (old and new)
- Executive / C-suite growth – individual and team
- Organisational reviews to reset the strategy and/or structure
- Plan and support change management (using neuroscience for change model)

THE MODEL AND METHOD

To achieve the perfect garden, you need to follow a few basic steps, use the right tools and techniques, have some patience, be encouraged by signs of growth and not too disappointed when it doesn't all go to plan. Be diligent with maintenance and ongoing development. So it is with a person, team or organisation.

It is key to note that the HEAD Gardener model does not exist on its own, there are many 'petals' or elements behind the 8 that we are focussing on which will make up the whole 'garden'. Nothing works in isolation from the other and in order to ensure that the head works in a person, so it is complemented by other features of the human, such as the body! Be that a fit and active one, or with differing levels of ability of a temporary or permanent nature. This model is one which work with the head, the model creates the outcome and it must be combined with the abilities in other areas of business function – such as operational efficiency, financial governance, technical skill and proficiency in whichever industry this is applied. It can be applied to any or all given a little thought.

The HEAD Gardener – Petal Model

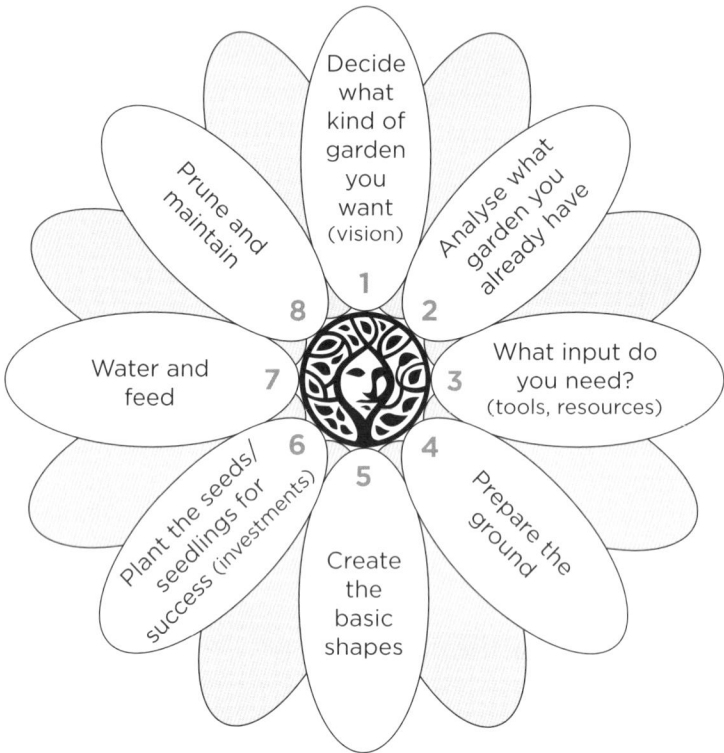

Overview Descriptor for The HEAD Gardener Petal Model

Although there is not a requirement to start from the first 'petal' when using the model in practice – as you may well have some aspects of the model already assessed, decided and designed, it is easiest to understand if we do.

1. **Decide what kind of garden you want** – the visioning, the idea of what the business will look like and the outcomes you are hoping to achieve, the product.

2. **Analyse what kind of garden you have now** – undertake an assessment of the positive and negative attributes you want to keep or remove from where you are currently, and your 'climate'.

3. Work out **what input you are going to need** (which gardeners knowledge you will need, what tools will be useful) and what you have already.

4. **Prepare the Ground** – including weeding out what you don't want and replanting, or for the compost, and adding hard landscape (boundaries, strategic objectives, requirements for the business).

5. **Create the basic shapes you want to plant in and their purpose** social area, productive garden, open areas for collaboration, and quiet reflection.

6. **Plant the Seeds / seedlings / plants** for success – make the investment in ensuring that you are only putting in what you need and want and in the right places.

7. **Water and feed** the plants (fertilizer) – investing in your teams, communications, giving support to those who need it the way they need it to grow.

8. **Prune and maintain** the garden – regular check ins and course corrections to manage how the garden is growing.

USING THE HEAD GARDENER MODEL

PETAL 1 – What Kind of Garden do you Want?

Vision is in essence the ability to see (and to create the vision of your business, career, or whatever the 'garden' is that you are focussing on). You need to picture the destinaion garden. You must unlock the creative in you, the going wild and dreaming big. Don't worry if it is not possible initially, if you feel ridiculous or simply think 'this isn't me', if you trust the process, you will get there. You may worry your ideas are too resource intensive, unachievable initially, that's ok too. We will deal with that later.

You can use traditional tools (forks and spades I call them,) such as the Disney coaching model – where each of the 3 processes of Dreamer, Realist and Critic all have their role to play in helping you come up with ideas, unrestrained and as broad as you can possibly imagine then go through the more logical planning and finally the barriers, risks etc to be overcome.

Another traditional method is to come up with a sentence that you can say in one breath that encapsulates what you are trying to accomplish. For example

"In a year I want to have a career that meets my commitment to support the environment and champions sustainability."

Or

"In 5 years I want to have purchased a house, be married and hope for a child…"

So now we know what a 'vision' is, how do you get one??

The most 'HEAD Gardeney' way of creating your vision is to dig deep into the garden model and come up with a picture or drawing (if you are arty), or maybe some descriptors of the garden that you can see in your mind's eye, where you point out the big showy flowers as key elements in your suite of products.

Or be practical, go and visit a garden – even by simply going outside, walk down the street and look at other peoples. How are you responding to what you see? What do you think and feel, see and admire or disregard…. By consciously looking at a garden you will see more and more layers, depth, different plants, perhaps the same garden is completely different at a different time of year or has colours that make you smile. Perhaps it has a theme or reference to a culture or homeland. Maybe it's a reclaimed bit of land from scrub and dust by the corner of a block of flats that has been planted and is being cared for. These are all responses to gardens and noticing someting real which was once only an idea.

Even if you haven't decided on the product or professional purpose of your life you might have some edges to it. You might like working with numbers, or mechanics, maybe economic theory combined with political trends, or maybe you enjoy the depiction of culture through art in its many forms. Whatever you are at you can begin to create your vision.

You might like to have a few ambitions – perhaps low level ones around 'making money while I sleep' type ideas that are the 'I want to do as little as possible for as much return as possible' and you can develop these plants or products, but I challenge you to consider whether that money will truly make you happier and more successful or is it just a hygiene factor for what you really want to do with your life? Perhaps you really want to create the financial sustainability for something, such as investing in your children (if you have any now or later) or even in the contribution to society.

One of the mistakes with visioning is that if you focus on making money first – 'chasing the dollar' – the purpose then comes second, and after a while the human brain needs more and more 'peaks' to give it the thrill of winning the cash! But if you start with the purpose based on a value you truly believe in, then the momentum to get up on the morning or try again after a failure will rejuvenate and be anchored in the core of who you are, not just the number is bigger than the last one… Of course, you want to be a success financially, I am not suggesting otherwise, but I am wondering if it truly grows you or is it a shorthand to get to the real priority? If it's all you have then all else has to take second place. Does that sit well for you? Maybe. It's your vision and choice.

Therefore, you need to decide the key aspects of your vision? Do you have a few core areas you want to work within and are you dreaming big enough, enough to think "I might or even could but really? Could I??" This challenges you about the size of 'garden' (vision, ambition) you want to create – and don't worry, you can always expand or reshape it later. Why not? That's evolution!

Choose if you are looking for a vision for the next year, or the next 10 years. If the former, you need to be very clear on the boundaries and scope of the vision to be achieved a year from today.

- How will the world be different?

- What will you notice?

- What will others say about you or your business?

Are you clear what the 'view' across the garden looks like in 1 year? Or if its 10 years, then thinking big, stretching the vision and then even a little more than you are comfortable with today will mean that as you stand looking at the garden in 10 years you will have a mature, evolved, well embedded garden, which has order, care, and the roots of what will be your legacy.... Is that what you are looking for?

Go back to the inspiring garden in your mind or that you have visited, what are the component parts? Does it have complementary colours and synergies between plants, perhaps those that follow on from one another, like a suite of products that you retail which have seasonal peaks in sales during the year.

Are you seeking to change the world in one go based on one purist product that you believe people need in their lives and you have the entrepreneurial drive to achieve?

Do you simply want a job that you enjoy, pays the rent, and opens doors to other parts of the world you have never even imagined?

Well, the good news is that gardens are that journey into new worlds, they can be curated and developed in small window boxes or plots of land or indeed they can be expansive and world changing.

Famous gardens and visions

I could write a whole chapter on famous gardens, from UK and across the world which would mean that this was a gardening book not a HEAD gardening book, and so I am choosing to pick out very specific references here to whet your appetite, in the hope that you will get the idea, feel stimulated to find your own sources of inspiration, and remember, exploring is part of the journey, so do check out your own ideas or those of others and see if they resonate with you. Simply ask 'Do you know a great garden? And 'what makes it great to you?' and you have yet another perspective on the development of your own.

Malcolm X had a dream, a vision, of 'a world where all [men] are equal' and used the phrase 'oasis' of freedom and justice, as an oasis is a 'garden' in the desert and indeed, he was referring to the state of Mississippi (as a desert state).

By the same token, the 'English Garden' became a vision as a more informal – yet structured – outside space which was more based in the landscape it belonged to rather than the ordered French Baroque style.

The Gardens of the Palace of Versailles outside Paris remain the most visited gardens to this day, and with all its grandeur. Yet in the UK our most visited garden is Sissinghurst, the home of Vita Sackville-West and Harold Nicholson (author and garden designer).

And then Singapore took gardens to another level – literally! Not content with a roof garden or a balcony, the Marina Bay Sands Hotel has a 'floating' garden above the hotel woven between the restaurants and observation deck.

In August 2023 The Times reviewed 11 of the UK most famous gardens for a number of key attributes and it made me think of the translation between type of garden and our areas of focus for growing people.

The Times Category of Garden	The HEAD Gardener Translation
Impressive variety	Diversity
Scientific history	Evidenced based action
Garden Inspiration	Leadership
Stunning Glasshouse	Supporting productivity
Fascinating Landscape	Creativity and Innovation
Giant Redwoods	Individual and Team Success
Impressive Topiary	Talent management
Historic Garden	Organisational memory
Peaceful Garden	Harmony through equality and inclusion
Botanical Wonder	Scientific genius
Mountain View	Strategic vision

So whether you know the parklands designed by Capability Brown at Blenheim Palace, or enjoy small scented quiet rose gardens more than formal gardens and extensive geometric parterres of Villandry in France, the key is to create the vision for your garden that brings you joy, focus and that you have a passion to work in.

Vison 'Plus'+

If you already have your garden – or product – then have you taken it to the next level? What's stopping you? I ask this only because plants and gardens – like humans or the moon – are either coming or going, they are either growing or they are dying, and so is your business or job growing or reducing in stature, interest, popularity or even your own desire to do the do!?

If you are looking to move on from your current garden to a new one, or looking to create a new 'room' to your current garden then the same rules apply, and take the walk, look around, visit a garden and see what inspires you to be more, different, change or add to refresh the place you are standing in. Then, you are ready for the next aspirations to be visioned and actioned.

PETAL 2 – What Kind of Garden do you have Now?

Stand in your own space. Just as you are. What is the world you are in? If it was a garden, what would it look like?

Are you a small border in a huge, landscaped garden? Or a medium sized productive garden supplying goods for others? Perhaps even an allotment with lots of other plots around you, but you know your berries are best yet you might have some yearning for a part of the flower cutting garden further down the slope?.....

The assessment of the garden you have today is similar to the visioning reflections and explorations from Petal 1, only this time it is the here and now. You can use all and every garden analogy here. Feeling pot-bound, being overgrown, gone to seed, tell me about your garden… tell yourself.

Attributes of the current garden

I often have people say to me *'Others recognise me for always supporting people, but actually I don't want to be only known for that, I want people to see I can lead well too'*

This next exercise is where you dig deep into your real self and notice that even if you are not using the skill at the moment it does not mean you do not possess it. You might have a superpower that others do not know about. This is the time to at least acknowledge to your yourself what that is. Also, time to have a look in the mirror and try and face up to the things that you know you do that are perhaps not the most attractive of your skills, and decide if you want to keep them, or if not, think about why you do what you do, and how you might 'dial down' some of their presence. Some professionals put on 'armour' to work in as they think they have to be seen as strong and serious, focussed and hard. Perhaps they do in certain circumstances. But maybe they don't need all that clanking metal and could just be themselves and people would respond better? And maybe these people only wear it for themselves as they have inner insecurities which they think others can't see if they wear an 'invincible' cloak or similar. But really? You can fool some of the people some of the time but not all of the people all of the time. So time to get real with yourself and get digging!

Exercise 2

Create a table like the ones on the following pages (or just use this one) with as many rows as you like. Then take a walk through your head garden.

What are you proud of that you do? Or if you really struggle with this, ask others what they think you are good at. This can be in the form of an informal 360 degree structure (those who work for you, your peers / colleagues, and a few more senior to you) You could look back at performance reviews, seeing if you agree with them (!) and what they might have missed that comes to your mind about what you know you are good at, but have yet to show perhaps.

And then take this to a deeper level of thinking in considering how these positive aspects of you serve you, what you like about them, and do you want to keep them?

Next, do the same with the negative attributes. How do they serve you? Why can't you let go of them? Do you secretly want to keep them?

Tables of Positive Attributes

	Positive Attribute	How does it serve you?
1		
2		
3		
4		
5		
6		

Tables of Negative Attributes

Negative Attribute	Can't let it go? Why not?
1	
2	
3	
4	
5	
6	

Now this is where you have to be both kind and ruthless.

My experience tells me that the reflection you have just undertaken will have gone one of two ways. Either, you will have been way too hard on yourself and made your positive attributes minimal and your negative ones the larger list, or you will have bigged yourself up to an extent that even you are sometimes wondering if you have gone a little far and might be super-stretching the truth… Familiar?

You need to decide what is true and neither hide in the shadows nor give yourself too much glory. Look again before you move on, and go back to the image of the garden. Because gardens neither lie, nor judge. Try the reflection of the visioning work in reverse. So not what kind of garden do I want to be, but 'if I described myself I would be a…' and then you might imagine a water garden with cool deep pools of knowledge or bubbling running water giggly in the brook and on your way to who knows what.

Or a rock garden, with your colourful attributes bedded into small pockets of hard rock, where you bring joy to others, but in the main want to (or do) look hard and impenetrable from the outside.

Perhaps you are a meadow garden, blowing in the wind, a few whisps of grasses making restful noises and calming others. Splashes of colour and a few generally hidden talents only to be enjoyed those who take time to look.

Maybe you are a big shouty blousy garden, with big floppy heads and colourful blooms?

Or are you the productive garden? The one with all the carrots in rows, planted next to the onions – as you like to have deep knowledge of the process before you commit to anything, and we know that carrot fly are put off by onions so that's where they are planted! Or neat rows of salad or vegetable which pleases your tidy mind.

You maybe need to give a plant or garden characteristics before you can take them or for yourself. You might find spikey plants are like spikey people or particular flowers that you don't even know the name of are pleasing because their blooms have symmetry. At this stage it doesn't matter. Just connect yourself with the characteristics of the garden and think about how they might describe your positive and negative traits.

What is serving you and driving you that you like? What are you good at, or like but don't need, on your next journey? It is perfectly normal to go from one area of emphasis to another.

Sometimes in your life you will be more leader than follower and sometimes more listener than speaker, and in the world that is your head as a garden you can enjoy the evolution of the seasons and your professional growth as you get deeper into the garden development. You do have to know what you are starting with to be able to create a path to your destination of the vision of the garden you seek.

As you begin this journey, and reflect with yourself or your team about what you might be as a community garden, do ask others what they see, and open the conversation to develop all those other senses. I recall a garden in Cyprus, where lying in bed one night the warm air gentle moved and swayed through the open window, and gusts of jasmine scent came in like a gentle caress. I inhaled, and then it was gone. I took another breath and it wasn't there. Then there is was again. Like willow-the-wisp coming and going and it made me feel that my life as a garden was at that moment peaceful, content and complete. And right then and there is was. The next day full of rest and peace I was able to go and do the work I was there for with a lightness of mind and heart, and whenever I feel the need to be still, and repaired, I know that garden scent is there and if I can find a jasmine the memory and the effect is exactly the same. So do find your garden that connects with you as you are.

PETAL 3 - What Input are you going to Need?

This section is all about the road map. You know where you want to get to in the vision of the garden and you know where you are and the garden that is you. So what's it going to take? And who and what will help – or detract!

We can all agree, I am sure, that gardening is likely to need some tools and techniques as well as some resources. Part 2 of this Beginners Guide defines a few of those, but in the model, the key part of this section is using what you already know or have, absorbing and implementing others knowledge and experience, and finally, using the right tools.

In your own head you have lots of experience and knowledge which will help you develop your new garden. You may have some ideas about what it will be like but not crystal clear yet, and that's ok, go round the cycle of the petals as often as you need to, your head garden like every other garden needs constant attention and will evolve.

So, what do you need for your garden?

What can you use that you have already grown. Perhaps your qualifications will be technically useful in your garden? Maybe you need to gain that qualification in order to create the new garden, or perhaps you could take a part of something you know and graft it onto another skill, perhaps take cuttings and plant up new little versions of the 'good bits' of you and then look further afield for support.

Example 1

I worked with a client who wanted to become a Chief People Officer across in a national public sector organisation. They had done it before in a different industry. The big question for him was 'how do I translate what I know I have done well to this new challenge?'

We undertook a review of the basic needs of the role, qualifications etc, and then looked into the scenarios of where his experience was relevant to solving some of this new organisations issues. We role played the hiring CEO's needs and his illustrations of what he felt he knew, where he had tackled such issues before, what would he do in a scenario he had not encountered before and then noted down where he had gaps, not in ability or will to achieve, but in the specific environment. After a lengthy exploration and some simple knowledge homework of learning the 'basics' of the industry – terminology, context and history of its growth, we agreed he would need a buddy / business mentor on achieving the appointment to the identified job, and as part of his recruitment preparation he made a very clear list of what he would need to 'hit the ground running' and what would take a little longer to absorb and experience. He shared this with the CEO in an informal conversation before the application so that all were clear on what support would be needed and available for his development, and you will be pleased to know he was the successful candidate.

Do you need others expertise, those who have been before you along the path? There is always some wise old quiet gardener in traditional gardens who looks like he was planted there along with the garden many a year ago, wearing earth-coloured clothes tied together with string, and gnarled hands and a favourite stubby knife? But these ancient gardeners can smell rain, feel the shifts in the land, see what the birds and insects do as the seasons change and it is their wisdom that we can translate into that of the mentor or one who has gone before that you need to learn from.

Who is that in your world? Look for those who are givers not takers, givers seek to help, but takers, well, they will eat your first hard won fruit. Yes, they tell you they are delicious but not a word for the excitement of those very early shoots or the wind and rain you went through to gain the first grown flower or bud. They are like cute looking pests! You forget they have their interests above yours, always, because they seem so endearing. Watch out for that in the garden and maybe invest in a scarecrow and some netting over your ideas so they don't get stolen!

Perhaps your HEAD garden needs some simple starter tools. It is indeed perfectly possible to make a hole in the ground or a pot with your finger to stick in a seed, or to pick off a deadhead between thumb and finger, but there are actually tools for these things which make the hole more consistent and the deadheading more efficient and less damaging to the plant. Who knew that the concept of gardening could also explain to us as 'professional humans' how to use the skill of Lean, or change theory, even financial – at least numerical – analysis!

In gardening itself, the 'starter kit' usually consists of

- Trowel (the garden version of a spoon or mini spade)

- Fork (just like the cutlery!)

- Gloves (you can, and should, simply feel the earth and all it has to offer us sometimes, but a little protection in some circumstances is a sensible move)

- Secateurs (these are a magical resource and come in all shapes and sizes but are basically, scissors. Snipping through tough stems, precision in removal of deadheads, or being just what's needed to cut or shear through some knottiness!)

You can get into spades, long handled forks, rakes, knives, dibbers, hoes, pruning knives and the like… but this is the Beginners

Guide, and we know, the expert tools of lifelong experience very rarely all come together at the beginning! So you might not need the super technical tool for your garden just yet and perhaps, let nature lead the way on this occasion.

You might also choose to remember a calendar, pencil and paper and a weather app! Not essential, but the sort of basic materials that help you remember what to 'plant' when, and when to expect results as well as notes of what you have already done – so you can look back on your journey and see what has worked or not. As for a weather app, well, this is the climate of your working environment. You could just 'look out of the window.' That would tell you how your garden is experiencing the professional 'weather' or you can use data and insight from the staff satisfaction surveys and communities within your environment, but it is a huge factor to take account of and one to be both acknowledged and understood – before seeking to change it.

One aspect that amused me in the development of this model for you, is that when testing it with a senior Director of a FTSE100 he became quite animated in this section – as he had big plans and wanted to create huge ambition with his 'garden' and asked me 'well wont I need planning permission for the walled garden?' which I have to say took the model one step further than I had even imagined. But this is your garden, your life, career, team, organisation and if you want to change direction or add and expand using this method you may well need to ask a few other people for their support or indeed permission! He wanted his 'start-ups' to grow and nurture and protect in his walled garden that would benefit from the irrigation coming from his vine house roof and other areas to collect water and he was, and is, building a successful and protective environment for some special new ventures using this HEAD gardening approach.

Three key questions

1. Who do you want to have input from in collecting the top tips or knowledge of those who have gone before in your gardening vision?

2. What knowledge do you already have to use and pay attention to more now that you have before in order to emphasise these aspects of you?

3. And what bits of 'kit' do you need to make it a reality, to protect your hands, your plants and help in breaking new ground for you.

Make some notes and perhaps discuss them in coaching conversations, team meetings or just to guide you.

So, what 'help' have you identified you need, from other people and from specific tools and techniques, knowledge and behaviours?

Remember to check the quality and quantity of what you already have! You didn't get to where you are on your own, but it is your journey and your success that you have been living with and cultivating.

One of the hardest things for some people to ask for, and often the best support you can receive, is help from others. If you have a vision, a dream or an idea then for others to help you is a big leap for you, and for them. For you, the 'helper' might not see the vision of your garden the way you do, might want to 'improve' it, criticise it, or simply not understand what you are trying to achieve. The helper themselves might feel either anxious to share ideas which would help hugely, or indeed be overbearing with their 'I've been there before' outlook and sharing – perhaps oversharing their vision rather than aligning themselves with yours.

The core principle of this petal in the model is to be brave in the ask and discerning in the use of the answers! You do not have to use the tool you have been offered, but if you don't know it exists, how will you know if it might help or hinder?

Let's take a look at two more examples, garden-based and organisationally effective to complete this petal.

Example 2

A successful public sector CEO wanted to become a Non-Executive Director (NED) in her field, so that she could ease back on the time and commitment to the sector but also use the investment of 40 years in that sector to help others. She had a fixed idea of the geography and 'flavour' of organisation – translated to the garden, she described her vision (Petal 1) for a productive vegetable garden not a flower garden or meadow. She knew what she knew (Petal 2) and she was committed to make the effort for Petal 4 (preparing the ground) but she didn't know what she didn't know!

In our conversations she came up with this action plan:

What I know I can offer / competency (Petal 2)

- Strategy development
- Operational leadership of teams
- Deep Finance specialist
- Understanding of assurance

What I need to know (help I need) (Petal 3)

- Focus on <u>challenge v support?</u>
- Chair and CEO <u>relationship?</u>
- <u>Other NED strengths</u>
- <u>Board commitment and committees</u>

Who I need to contact to test my thinking

This was a list of people, some of whom were NEDs, others Chairs and included those outside her own sector

What have I not thought of (fill in later)

New Ideas!

LEAVE BLANK IN CASE!

Whilst the actual plan was longer than the outline shown here, there are some key areas of help / tools she identified she needed to explore:

- Challenge v support = frames for operating, be they bamboo poles, a wall to lean on or making sure the 'productive garden' was being encouraged to grow but given help

- Relationships = a healthy relationship between plants, and even 'the carrots and onions being planted together warding off carrot fly' are all about ensuring that the human factors (or living creature factors!) work together and not suffocate one from another or simply try and 'go it alone'

- Other NED strengths = recognising the benefit of pollinators, such marigolds and flowers of the vegetables in order to create the 'fruit'.

- Logistics = Boards and committees, timelines, is simply the seasonal planting plan. Knowing when to sow the seed, when to thin out, when to add feed (more later in petal 7) and when to expect the maturing of some and the time to replan for the next year.

Example 3

A senior military officer retiring from their role aged 55 wanted to achieve a second career in leading an organisation with a public service ethos. He felt confident in his own environment (as most mature plants do!) and in his seeking of a new challenge, but one where his skills would be used, he wanted to find out what he knew he didn't know. We therefore came up with the list of 'Appreciative Inquiry' questions for him to positively explore his 'garden'.

Here are some examples in supporting his 'Petal 3' focus;

- *What does the garden look like that I have enjoyed most (the strategic focus of discovery and appreciation) (Petal 2)*

- *What more, different or the same do I want in this next garden? (dreaming / innovating) (Petal 1)*

- *What other gardens are out there that I have knowledge and experience to deploy (Petal 3)*

- *How have others moved from one garden to another at my stage in life (Petal 3)*

- *Who do I know and respect who has created a new garden? (Petal 3) What have they learnt in their journey?*

- *Do I need to 'dig deep' and reinvent myself or can I use some of my current 'soil and structure' (environment) to re-plant a new garden?*

- *What are my basic tools – a spade, a knife and string (aka my will to work hard, my ability to make decisions and my ability to create connections and keep them together)*

- *What more do I need?*

  - Some netting = air cover / financial stability to start the growing of something new and not be eaten by passing pests!

  - Secateurs = cut off some of the previous roles I have held or am known for

  - Watering can = a few allies who will promote my growth (and buy me a drink when I need it!)

  - Specific seeds = area of expertise that I can grow, propagate and achieves the outcome I am seeking

This individual is now a Chief Operating Officer of a Global Building & Design firm.

PETAL 4 – Prepare the Ground

In this chapter we explore some of the clearing of the ground and mind in order to have the ideal conditions to receive the ideas of the vision you have created and all its potential. This is one of my favourite parts of gardening a head! This is where you are clear exactly what it takes to 'GO' after you have done the initial 'getting ready' phase.

First, look back for a moment on where you have come from. You know what you want to do (the vision) you know what you have (the assessment of you now), you know what you need (self and others help) to create the garden, and now you can really start to get your hands dirty by clearing away all that will not serve you as you begin to create.

So what does the ground – your head – look like? Is it cluttered and weedy? Have brambles of self-doubt and thorns of anxiety been spiking you? Or are you already wielding the tools of grubbing out and chopping away all those old, unnecessary ugly factors that will slow you down and you no longer want to be careful of, but rather rip out and burn so you can get on with your life in your way to deliver your vision and a blossoming growthful and developing future.

Perhaps you think you are right ready to go and don't have any weeds. You have a green field site that is ready for you to dive into with your designs and then plant. Watch out! This is common mistake. Just because you cannot see a weed or plant above ground does not mean its not there, it means you can't see it. You MUST dig over the ground, even if you think you are confident, competent and know exactly what your plan is. By not doing so you will not know what nasties lurk beneath the surface. Those people you think are with you, support you, nod at the right moments… Are they really? Or are they telling you what you want to hear and when push comes to shove they will melt away due to their own fears or favours. Trust is the core element of this chapter. Yes, there is the preparation of the clearance of irritating areas of focus in your life that you need to let go of, leave, end, finish, stop, so that there is space to grow this new life, but there is also the testing of the richness of the soil that you are about to plant it. Who will stand with you when all else falls away?

I have found that it is very rare to be able to come up with a plan for your next chapter and deliver it exactly as you had intended – which may be a good thing, sometimes. But if you have not 'mulched', 'enriched' and refined that which you are starting with then I am here to tell you that your head, business, team or ambitions will not grow as strong and sustainably as you have the vision for.

What is business compost?

At its basic compost in general is the breaking down of nutrients from matter that has gone before and is then broken down to return to the earth and can provide food and 'goodness' from its having simply 'been'. What is interesting in compost is that – unless you are a truly high-end gardener winning prizes with your produce – most compost for the normal gardener comes from normal grass cutting and weeds. And this makes me smile. Yes, we need to remove toxic and poor behaviours from the workplace, now more than ever, but we also need to learn from these people and unfortunate experiences and pass on that learning, knowledge and better role modelling to the next generation as we now know better and have had the opportunity to remove the badness and use it to create a better outcome for future growth.

I came across a new-ish compost maker which piqued my interest because not only will it take pretty much anything from a natural source and 'cook' it as it breaks down into a liquid form that you can dilute and use as a fertiliser, but it also does it all by itself, and become a 'hot house' of goodness. It made me think of managing talent and the intensity of making the strongest of nutrients to then be absorbed by the soil which in turn will give it to the plants to help them grow and achieve their potential and beyond.

Preparing the ground therefore means digging in, or using, some of the 'business compost', some of the learning dug into your ground to make sure you have the best possible chance for success.

There are a number of schools of thought in gardening about whether or not you should dig over the soil and when, and yes it can oxygenate the ground, but it can also break up some of the soil structures that knit together to bond and be 'strong' as a soil that holds together and holds up the plants. My preference is to 'oygenate' to begin with, to provide a bit of looseness in the soil and manages the water deluge and dry times, not necessarily digging down too deeply and unearthing too many emotions or looking back to far, but to provide some lightness to the current situation, and an 'ease' with myself and with those I am working with to be warmed up and ready to make progress with the next stage.

Big plant preparation!

I must confess, there is something very satisfying about getting the big digger out and simply carving into and chucking away some of the old and unneeded aspects which are unhelpful to a new garden.

Some of these are experiences where we haven't been treated well at work, or we have felt undermined by others. Perhaps someone has diminished your confidence, or you have missed out on training, opportunities or, as you feel it, been the victim of bullying. All of this might be true. However, if you are to create a vision for your new garden, know where you are at, get the tools together and start the preparation then why on earth would you give any of these people or businesses any more of your energy?

They have served their purpose; it has not been a positive experience but now is the time to get that big digger out and get rid of them. Don't carry them. Do not fear that their power is more than yours, and it certainly isn't as great as they will have you believe. You are the one who has a vision, a garden to grow and those weeds and thorns that hurt you are of no use to you except as compost for your learning. So, this is the stage where you let go, chuck them on the compost heap and use the nutrients of those lessons which have been hard learnt!

Preparing others

I have a view that most people look like they are listening but a maximum of only 50% of them actually are. So, when you turn round and say 'I am going to create a new garden' or 'I am moving on (job/role/life)' they are rather surprised and taken aback. Its not that they didn't mean to listen, or even did listen but then forgot – perhaps had weeds of their own to contend with, and so needed to pay attention to that rather than you. It is your job to help them really hear where you are going, what the ambition is, and what they can do to help – including getting out of the way!

'Others' come in many different shapes and sizes, family, friends, colleagues – peers, followers and leaders and each needs their own preparation. If your family know you best then the preparation may be an expected move where you have already shown 'indicators and warnings' of change. If not, this is the stage to have that conversation! Change for you will always mean change for those in your life, and whether it be good or bad or simply different, I find a smoother path if others are aware. You don't need to take account of their opinion (see Petal 3) but if they are to ensure you have a clear path then they wont know this unless you tell them!

Those who have a vested interest – friends, or trusted colleagues, they are part of the preparation as by sharing, they will be ready to lend an ear, again, and again! They will also challenge and check-in that you are getting what you really want. This is not a 'nice to have' this is something that you will need to fall back on, return to, or ask of, and if you feel the seeds aren't growing fast enough or the 'weather' is spoiling your growth, it is these people who you have prepared to stand by you and help you work out what you can do and not sit in the misery of what you can't!

Professional colleagues need a different sort of preparation. You need to decide who you can trust, and conversely who will steal your ideas, who are the smiling assassins, who are the joyless Eyores, the doom mongers and those who reflect their own inadequacy onto you and crush your preparation for your new and better garden. Sadly this mainly comes from jealousy, and others insecurity, but there will be those who you CAN trust, who will follow you to the ends of the earth because you can be trusted, you inspire them and you know they have your back.

These are the people to prepare. Don't waste energy on the others, but on those who you know you care about and who care about you. They will be there through all the seasons not just the sunny days.

When you have prepared yourself, your family, friends and colleagues its time to create the basic shapes and designs of your new garden.

PETAL 5 – Create the Basic Shapes and Designs

As an organisation this is an essential part of the garden. All aspects can evolve and grow and come in and out of emphasis, but the basic shapes and designs really are the 'hard landscaping' of your garden. As a person or team these are the rules, which keep everyone pointing in the agreed vision direction and not demurring.

You have your vision, you know where you're at, you know what you need for the journey ahead, the preparation is complete and now you can get to work on the strategy, the boundaries, hard edges, the soft flowing of some borders into others or whatever it is that will be underpinned by the architecture and scaffolding of this section to give strength and reality to the intention. One of the unsung heroes of design is also the freedom and creativity that can be explored when being underpinned with the strength of clarity.

For humans we tend to find pleasure in symmetry and balance, and find this calming in a garden, and yet we can also enjoy surprises and unusual aspects we weren't expecting – although these are not restful and restorative, rather stimulating and an exciting frisson in our heads where order is usually intended, and it is not a surprise by this stage in the model that it is also true of HEAD gardening.

Most of the time we enjoy a status quo, and a time of balance with the odd peak and trough where we can develop and enjoy new things as well as the familiar ways of doing things. There is nothing wrong with having hard landscaping which is a very uniform shape and one which has no surprises, we are all different and linear development is great if that's your thing. For some, however, a bit of 'mixing it up' works, although most enjoy this when it comes underpinned by a few certainties. We say we like freedom, but I believe from all those I have met that we like freedom within boundaries, so we don't scare ourselves silly!

If you take the principle of good garden design; proportion, transition, and unity, and apply them to your head garden, then you will find that you can create the 'rooms' in your garden or the career, give structure to elements and freedom to others, and then create a way of transitioning between them because all of the garden you create is you. You are completely 'you' whichever way you look! So you need to transition from one part of yourself to another at different times, and in a way that feels congruent to you. And that congruence is the unity. In an individual it is inner peace and quiet, contentment, satisfaction. In a team, unity will bring harmony where each makes their contribution to the whole, so the whole delivers more than one person or aspect of the garden. And for the organisation, the equality, inclusion and proportionality of action / inaction, a space for innovation and a time for focus, all come from the proportional response and responsibility that good design in the HEAD garden can provide.

Look even more closely, as there is always more to see of a living being than at first appears, including in a garden. The longer you look, and notice, there are contrasts between people be that diversity of shape, colour, purpose or history. These contrasts and compliments between one another are reflected in the garden where the use of contrast, alignment and proximity is one of the ways in which we design a place that connects with us as other living beings. Repetition in planting can bring a rhythm to our borders or our lives, and that repeating pattern that we recognise in a 'ah, yes, you again' way brings familiarity to us, and through familiarity, comfort. So it is with the HEAD garden. The familiarity that our structure and rules give us the basic shapes of our garden. If you are creating your own garden and wanting to develop a new way of thinking, curating and developing then you can create your own shapes, designs, and it is the principles of the garden design that can be captured to create that growth in yourself, team or organisation.

In truly structural terms for the organisation I recommend also using these design principles for people spaces, such as open spaces for collaboration, more enclosed quiet reflection areas or formal / informal contrasting parts of a business which help people thrive – more light or water, more energising noise, or less so. HEAD Gardening and its principles can grow your people in all settings at work with a little application.

Taking these principles and structural ideas into practical business or personal development terms might feel like a big step, but just like drawing the garden you want to create you can draw the outlines and shapes of how you would like your life or organisation to be.

For example; here is a person who has designed their life to have spiritual growth as the corner stone and surrounding support for their family, with some friends from that group and some not, where work feeds the family and the spiritual growth supports them in their work, where there are professional social occasions but not connected to their family life and where the focus of outdoor activities are a main feature connected to some voluntary work and some not, but not related to family.

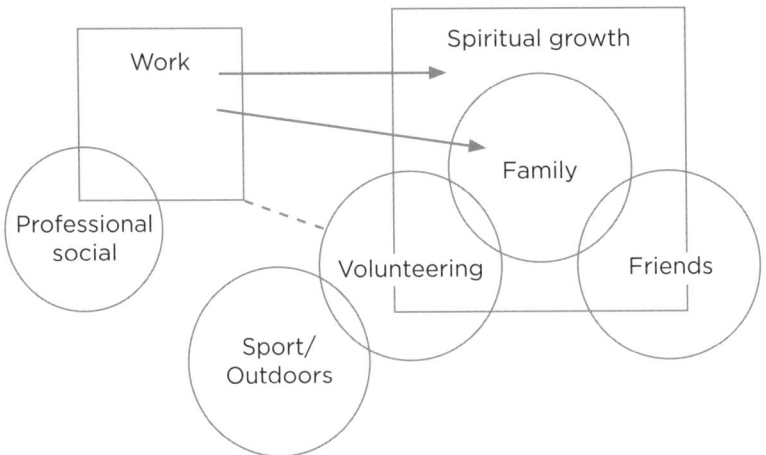

Here is another person who looks at the design of their new garden – having arrived at a new organisation and setting the vision to achieve Executive Director / C-suite status in 3 years. Here they are focussing on increasing technical knowledge, developing more sensitive emotional intelligence, building relationships and managing their time, in order to deliver excellence in their current role, which will lead them to apply for the 'Next Director Programme' in one year, fulfil that by end of year 2 and apply for a C-suite role in year 3.

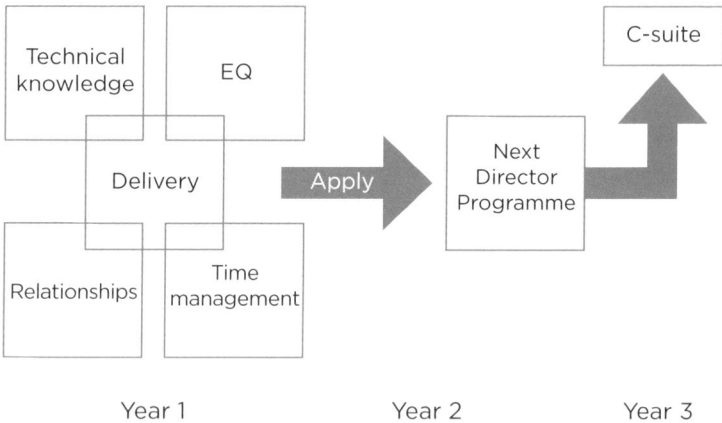

| Year 1 | Year 2 | Year 3 |

With a little attention to the underpinning frame for your achievements you always have a place to 'go back to', to return to somewhere familiar in your thinking and plans, and then go again, go differently, or go further in your ambitions.

PETAL 6 – Planting

One of fun parts of HEAD gardening – and gardening itself – is deciding what goes where, how plants will complement one another, and enjoying the journey of planting a seed and then seeing the story unfold as it grows and thrives. Here our mantra is 'cultivating success' and making the right investments in order to ensure you are only putting in what you need and want, and vitally, where you want them.

I look at this chapter as being divided into three sections;

- planting seeds,

- potting on seedlings,

- choosing where the plants go
  (positioning in the environment of the garden).

Then we flip the principles and tasks into how this is mirrored in an attraction, recruitment and retention cycle for you, your teams and organisations. I include talent management and leadership development and share some cautions around cutting corners or having expectations not conducive with what you have asked of your people, or plants, and what to do then!

Let's start at the beginning.

Before you do ANYTHING else, *'dig some organic matter into the soil to give the roots chance to thrive'* so says the Gardener Adam Frost. We know this if we have prepared the ground (Petal 4). The same is true for people and if you have a rubbishy old office with an unwelcoming front of house team, the ID badge isn't ready and HR aren't expecting the new arrival on Day 1 it's not a great way to say 'hurrah! Glad you joined us'… It's the organisation organic matter you need to have ready as don't forget the 'newbie' chose you as much as you chose them!

Planting seeds

In your head, imagine yourself with a pot or container in front of you, and you are going to plant some seed or bulb to grow into multiple flowers. You don't just chuck in the seed, or maybe a few, stick some soil on top, splash of water and then hope for the best. Yet why is it that we so often choose a seed – or person – to join our team and have high hopes for their success, production and beauty, and we do just that! Where are the holes at the base of the container to let the water through and not become waterlogged? What about choosing one seed for one container instead of tipping a group of people into a team and hoping they'll sort themselves out? Why do we drop any old soil on top of them, call it nutrition and expect that soil – or training – to magically help them grow. And what about the water? There is a whole chapter on that! But it is essential for human life and all life, and yet, that essential ingredient for professionals to thrive is all too often missing, humankind, the actual being of a human. We are all born with empathy and a neurological ability to care, but how, and if, we nurture it either helps this grow or wither away.

Worse still, we know this! We know that if we had a seed to plant in a garden that we had chosen we could have no such expectation of it that we give to ourselves and our people, so how do we change this. What should we do!?

Firstly, dwell a pause. Take a breath.

Planting is an act of faith, as it is with recruiting a new person to your team, or contracting with an organisation to deliver your requirement. We make the decision to choose a person and then we look to them to thrive. Sometimes we provide mentors – like supports in a garden setting, sometimes we check in regularly and are available as leaders for people to raise concerns or questions, but mainly, we fool ourselves that it will be ok and work itself out.

You wouldn't do that to vegetables if your wellbeing depended on eating them would you? So now we know this, let's do it differently.

To plant as a HEAD gardener, there are ways of choosing plants or young plants carefully. You have to know what you are looking for its true, but if you look for the potential of a person and the intentions you have to grow them then that combination is far more likely to succeed than any other type of myth and magic. When a small seed shows one then two leaves and shoots of promise, do not rip it out of its cosy pot and stick it in an enormous border. However strong it looks, predators like succulent green shoots, and will devour it. And the person or seedling will be lost, not be able to fight for the light and eventually give up. Therefore, pot it on, to a pot which is bigger, presents more challenge, perhaps add some nutrients (more anon) and keep and eye on it to ensure it is doing ok!

Potting on

It is really easy to become pot bound once you have promoted once – either as the promoter or promoted. This is because as a seedling you had (or not!) the support, and you survived, grew and felt that bigger space and greater freedom and responsibility that being a medium sized plant gave you. As a promoter you now expect your people who have grown to then seek promotion or you can assume that they are happy where they are – wrong! As the promoted you assume that either you will be picked for the next role or promotion when you are ready and your boss will see this, and that in some magic way they know how much you have grown and that you are ready for the next step, or pot, and so why would they not give you the next promotion or role, you're ready for it after all! Also wrong.

This potting on business is all about communication. Some grow quicker than others, some are happy in a role (or pot) for far longer than others, even if they could move on they don't want to but are content to flourish in the confines of their current environment, but for those who have decided that growth and success are their watchwords, do not let their roots grow out of the bottom of the pot and anchor themselves into the deeper ground they sit on! If a person or plant is determined to grow, there is very little you can do to stop them, so why not help and nurture them so that when they are the largest shrub in the border they can perhaps provide some shade from the scorching sun for the newer, younger and more vulnerable plants as they begin to grow. Others success should never be feared but encouraged. As a result all learn and all grow.

For those who simply want the reward for themselves and worry they will miss out by helping others grow, that is their choice, but they will find that as they become woody and out of date, the younger and more succulent plants will be less inclined to save them from the storms and brittle twigs do tend to snap off in the high winds so you have been warned!

Planting position

Choosing for yourself what kind of role and position you want in a garden is never a certain task, but there are a few principles to follow in making these choices, such as;

- Days in the sunshine (or fame / highly visible role) can be very pleasant, but also tiring if you don't have respite from time to time. Balance is important.

- No job / decision is forever and the environment, role, or your desires may change. So make your choices with what you know, have found out, and can see from here, not conjecturing what life will look like in years to come.

- Choose an environment that suits you. Most plants can survive in most soils, but they thrive in those that suit them best. If you prefer a fast-paced driven high octane environment don't choose a sleepy hollow to put your roots down!

- Keep hydrated! Particularly in the early days. This is for both plant – person – and gardener. It is important to ask questions, lots of them, and learn the lie of the land as soon as possible, and for the gardener, keep checking in on your new arrival, you don't want them drying out while they try and establish themselves in the team / border!

One of the other key times where planting plants and position is most important, and indeed most emotive, is in times of change and restructure in any organisation. The underlying issue is security and status, but it shows up as process blocking, poor behaviour and searching for alternatives, all of which is based on the emotional pain being felt by those involved (See 'Energy Rising' – Julia DiGangi) in any type of negative sensation being experienced.

Whilst processes are likely to be 'fair' in organisations in restructure, due to the requirements and protections that employment legislation and protection have brought about, there may be feelings of injustice and emotional damage to someone who wants/wanted a position and doesn't get it when the final decisions are made, or carelessness of the implementation of the process leading to mistakes and frustrations. Here the plant positioning is at its most tricky and needs the most care. Work out – preferably in consensus – and with those involved, who will thrive best where, and MOST importantly, who will help the business thrive best. You may find that the brassy marigold might not be in and of itself one of the plants you might choose initially but they are great pollinators attracting insects by their bright colour, and perhaps you need a few of them to help the others thrive. Do not go for all those who wish to be the star of the show, use up all the nutrients, are glorious for a blink of an eye and that's it for the rest of the year….. balance, as ever, is the key word in considering change and positioning of your 'plants' and teams/team members.

PETAL 7 – Water and Nutrients

You might think you know what water and nutrients do. In gardens – as Lucas Phillips said back in 1952 – *"Cultivation begins with drainage, a sine qua non…"*

He goes on to say;

"To all normal garden plants, a water-logged soil is fatal. The soil must, of course, be capable of holding such moisture as the plants need – and some need a lot – but excess water must be able to drain away. In most existing gardens today, there is little that need be done, but in new ground, or in major operations such as terracing, a drainage operation is likely to be necessary."

If you think about applying this premise to people in organisations and where 'water' is replaced by the words and actions of 'support' the sentence still stands up. It is true that most people will go and find what need to get the support they need to undertake their role, but some may not, and it is these more gentle and unassuming specimens that will not survive in your organizations climate and may wither to a shadow of their former selves and lose the faith in themselves of that which they once had potential for.

We know that 70% of a human is water and it is not a dissimilar percentage of a human that needs other human care, empathy and interaction with others. So if human support and contact is our 'water' then it is vital to our very professional existence, even before we seek to thrive, we need to survive!

So what is the 'water' / support that we can offer to one another?

As a basic human right we have the right of everyone to an adequate standard of living for themselves and their family, and that includes the right to water. It may not be an absolute 'right' in a professional sense, but we do accept that a basic standard of behaviour, opportunity and growth should be afforded to us by our professional life, and I would argue our non-working life too.

If water – support – is that important, then what is it that is so vital to you in your 'HEAD garden' as an individual, team or organisation??

- A sense of belonging?
- Opportunities to learn new skills?
- Taking action with a level of autonomy?

And sometimes it is the consistency or rhythm of those moments where you give or receive feedback, where you add to your knowledge – little by little, where you have healthy human contact and feel safe in the leadership to offer or experience.

For the water of our professional life – just as in a garden – we need to have the right amount, at the right time, and be able to drain the excess away where it does not serve us. We need to create the environment where that drainage happens, and where we have planted well so that those who require more, get more, those who require less are not water-logged but thrive in their best environment, as that brings both an effective individual in delivery of your desired output as well as them enjoying the experience, therefore thriving and growing even more.

Types of water/ support and their uses:

Looking deeper into the types of water or support you might need in your garden, there is that which comes without asking – such as the rain, when sometimes you are glad for it and other times not! You need to ensure that the input / learning or 'deluge' of the rain is something that you can be more deliberate about than wondering when and where and how you will receive this 'water' from the sky. Do note that there is usually someone who can forecast the rains, to different levels of accuracy, but if you pay attention and seek to become knowledgeable about when the rain / support will come, then you can decide whether you want to go out in it or not! That is having the agency to choose to soak up the new water, information, way of working, or keep under shelter.

Another type of water that comes to mind is the use of 'wastewater' or 'grey water'. This has some of the properties of the nutrients of fresh water but has been used before by someone else. We often want new and untouched versions of knowledge but in this instance where there has already been one use for the water there can easily be more, recycled, and learnt from water. Learning from others' experiences, even if they seem unrelated to our own can often bring a new perspective, add to us in a way we hadn't even thought of, and we grow in new and unexpected ways.

There are waters which are bad for some plants – peas, beans and roses are damaged by salt, yet mangroves and some of the prickly pears love it or at least tolerate it. As with all inputs to our garden in our head, we have to be decide what the 'water' of our life is for us, the support we need to thrive, and the regularity we need it.

The mechanism to receive support is also something to consider. For watering a garden, you can range from watering can to hosepipe right the way through to an irrigation system – or just rely on the rain to fall. However, in the water that is our support, we have a number of mechanisms which we can use to grow ourselves and our learning which suit us more appropriately than others – be that because of time, capacity, learning style preferences or budget!

Courses, coaching, reading, watching videos, talks, YouTube, TEDtalks, formal degrees like a Masters, MBA, even a doctorate are all ways to be fed the water of your growth. We know that adults grow best through experiential, coaching and formal teaching in the proportions of 70:20:10 and yet many of us do not seek fresh water from shadowing others, observing our bosses bosses boss with a curiosity, or even acknowledging that we still need water at all!

Successful leaders of people, who tend their garden and keep it flowering year after year, producing the crops from the veg patch, know what their people need and ensure they have it. They also know what they need to be refreshed to grow their knowledge, seek new horizons and grow so they continue to thrive. They must prune and maintain their own skills (see Petal 8) and they continue to consistently 'water' themselves, challenge their assumptions and listen, hear and then take action.

6 Questions to Ask Yourself:

- What is the water / support that you need to grow right now?

- Are there other types of water / support that you can identify that you might also need?

- How often do you need it?

- What happens when you don't have the support you need?

- How do you / can you access support?

- What can you do to share it to help others thrive too?

Nutrients

As we continue to consider support and the nourishment of ourselves, teams and organisations, lets take a look at what 'nutrients' you might like to add in – and are already within you! – to aid your growth in the garden.

What are they?

A nutrient is *'any substance that plants or animals need in order to live and grow'* (Cambridge Dictionary).

For gardens, there are 3 main fertilizers or nutrients. Nitrogen – which helps stem and leaf growth, Phosphorus which helps in seed formatting and stimulating root growth, and Potassium which promotes the flowers then fruits. There are many other minor ones, but these 3 are the basics. They can be either organic or chemical.

For our own 'HEAD gardening' there are also many fertilizers which do different jobs! And they can be organic or specifically manufactured to assist us (just as vitamin supplements are for humans too!). Some of the human nutrients for growth in our context are;

- **Respect** – grows our understanding of those around us and hear other perspectives
- **Inclusion** – grows our community and connection to others
- **Opportunity** – grows our capability to learn new skills or enhance those we have
- **Feedback** – grows our ability to reflect on how we are experienced by others
- **Security** – grows our confidence to keep striving and growing

When / how do I use them?

Some of our human nutrients for HEAD gardening are easier to come by than others, some we have in greater abundance already and some we need to seek out. But all can be added to your daily life and enhance your ability to grow and achieve your goals. We also need different ones for different circumstances.

Let's look at 3 examples where we need to replenish our nutrients and how we do this – using the garden.

1. **Natural replenishment** – There are natural way of replenishing nutrients in a garden from leaving the soil fallow for a season and not asking anything from it, or crop rotation or mixed cropping are also other ways of bringing variety and different asks to refresh the soil. Sound familiar? Of course, leaving our 'HEAD garden' fallow is often easier said than done, but techniques such as mindfulness, more sleep and a gentle 'taking your foot off the gas' can all be restful and rejuvenate us.

2. **Experiential** – by trying new ways of working, or working with new people, we can experience new approaches to work that we think we thought we knew. For example, if our professional focus is on continuous improvement, we might have one method that we know if useful, but there are many more based on similar attributes but modelled and ordered differently. Using a familiar base, reaching out to try a new model or way of delivering a project or change programme might provide your own lightbulb moments and help you learn and grow from others. You might also seek to pilot a new idea in a small way in your team to see if the benefits can be realised, and this experience of exploration can create the new input and fresh growth of learning that you seek – as well as a positive result!

3. **External inorganic method** – this is mainly around applying new knowledge or skill. You have had the input of learning / training / developing a skill from some new knowledge and now you apply it in your role. Whether it's a personal development insight or a technical skill is not important, what matters is that you are absorbing a new piece of information and then you apply it logically in your professional setting.

All examples are given to show how to absorb the nutrients and each will be used in different moments and settings. This is where your consider what you need to enhance your growth and choose a way of absorbing the nutrients you need.

We should also notice ways by which we lose our nutrients. How do we lose them? In all agricultural systems (bigger than gardens), nutrients are removed over time in harvested products, such as grain, and there can also be a diminishing health of soil occurring through erosion, runoff, leaching and burning of crop residues. Often by feeling excluded, uncertain, lacking opportunity, becoming pot-bound (see Petal 6) and not working on our resilience we can also feel eroded, diminished and our nutrients ebb away. This means that either by our own acts or those of others, we are less likely to grow and begin to struggle, shine less, and everything is more effort and less joyful.

So, to achieve a healthy 'HEAD garden' – for you or your team – nutrients are an important part of growing and sustaining its lifeforce.

What do these nutrients achieve?

Happy healthy inclusive respectful gardens invite feedback and feel secure, so thrive even more than before. Nutrients in and of themselves in our context have been considered to some as 'soft skills' or aspects of work that are not the main effort. However, without them naturally occurring, being part of 'how we do things round here' or without additional input, the landscape and environment you seek to plant your ideas or new products in simply will not be appropriately nourished.

We have probably all heard of tomato feed? This is the liquid 'stuff' that is known to create a better quality and quantity of the crop of tomatoes. However, you don't use it straight away from planting the tomato seed nor when it is super small as it is so strong you might burn the roots, but when it has begun to get going you can then feed it regularly. Like children moving from milk to solids, or like people growing in their professional life moving from consciously incompetent to unconsciously competent..

Jones Loflin a speaker and author of *Always Growing*, tells a story about a man who has leadership struggles and finds clarity in his sisters' gardening business in the US. Loflin uses the analogy only for leadership roles, however I see that every employee, member of a team, and in fact human being needs the nutrients of feeling seen, heard and understood in order to stay healthily connected to the community around them. It is these 'nutrients' that stop the human from becoming desiccated and exhausted, lonely and often burned out or depressed or both. Remember, devoting time and access to your peers and team members is in and of itself a powerful nutrient and achieves your growth, and your subsequent flowering and fruiting into a stronger higher quality – and happier! – specimen in your garden.

PETAL 8 – Prune and Maintain

Looking after yourself and cutting off or out bits of your life that you no longer need is the essence of this petal.

Where once we needed our early wins, examples of achievements and successes, as we get older and more experienced some of them begin to matter less or are overtaken by bigger and better 'branches'. Now is the time to prune. Gardeners know that there is a time and a season for pruning different plants and so it is with our human HEAD gardening. The key is not just timing, but how much to chop off in order to achieve better, stronger, more prolific growth!

Starting with the garden, there are many sage old (and new) gardeners that will write books on this very subject, at length, for every different sort of fruiting tree, bush, shrub, flowers and anything else you can think of. One of my gardening icons, Monty Don, has 13 references to pruning in The Complete Gardener! Yet I am, on this subject at least, with Lucas Philips in his anchoring his expertise on this subject, by quoting Shakespeare's Gardener in Richard III who talks of pruning as:

"Superfluous branches we lop away, that bearing boughs may live"

It's all about enhancing the next period of growth. So, we will look at when, where, and how to prune your HEAD garden and what to look out for so you don't cut out potential buds of growth by accident!

When?

The question of pruning tidying and maintaining the effort and outcome to deliver against the vision you began in Petal 1 comes at a time when you have had some success, understood some of the planting pleasures and flourishes of achievements, as well as realising some of your less brilliant moments! There is a whole series on 'failing fast' with Amy Edmondson, so I won't labour that point here, but rather, share some principles to know when to prune elements to then go on and continue to grow and thrive.

The cycle of flowering or creating fruit and then pruning is something that is eminently transferable to us. And its different for each of us. Some of us produce flowers and then need deadheading – yes, this is a form of pruning to encourage further flowers from the same plant. Think of Sweet Peas or Cosmos, they think they are being 'attacked' so in their 'fight or flight' they bang out some more blooms to keep being valuable. Then they go over. You chop them off. More come. But if I was an apple tree, if you chopped off my blossom then there would be no pollination and no apples. So, apple trees are pruned after fruiting.

The answer to the question 'when' to prune therefore depends on your growth cycle. Have you come to a period in your career or life, or even in the leadership of the vision you began with to grow your garden and find that there are aspects of the business that have grown more than you would like and some that haven't done so well, either because of others or for other reasons, but this then takes you on to where to prune.

Where?

Here you need to make some decisions. Check back to Petal 1, is it what you still are seeking to achieve? Have you achieved it? Is it 'maturing nicely' – so that Petal 2 is more aligned to the vision than when you started? By having continuous and high quality input from Petal 3, and ongoing ground preparation, structure, nurturing and care (Petal 4,5,and 7) your choices in Petal 6 have come to fruition (we hope!) so this is really the moment you reflect and make the preparations for the next stage of growth.

There will be aspects that have become more overbearing than you would like. Or have grown off shoots (spending time on pet projects?) which you don't want, perhaps which are detracting from the main business? Are there some of the departments which have completely overshadowed others and are absorbing all the time and 'light' from others and yet are not adding SO much value by being so big?

Perhaps its time to cut back a few plants or characters that have become a little overbearing and 'legends in their own lunchtime' and whom are either power-hungry, mood-hoovers or if you look closely are manipulating the business or service to work for their entire satisfaction and not the other way around? Time to prune.

Pruning might be seen as a punitive activity for humans, and for some it is a 'course correct' but in the main it is shaping and preparing for the next season of growth. The idea is to propel the living being into the next season of growth whilst not having them damaged by the forthcoming seasonal changes, time of year, weather or strategy of the firm they are loyal to.

If you have a personal 'HEAD garden' that you are seeking to 'prune' then ask yourself this question;

What are you spending most of your time doing (professionally), and what is giving you the most joy / return on your investment?

The answer to this question will tell you whether you are growing and are spending the time on the right activities to give you the results you are looking for, or if you are growing without aim. If the latter, the time to go back to Petal 1 and have a think about what you really want to achieve. If the former, then perhaps also go back to Petal 1 to create an even more ambitious vision of your next garden, to plan the expansion of this one, and consider how you might help others with theirs.

How?

Its all very well to have the theory of what to do and when to do it, but if you don't know how then chances are you either won't do it at all, or you'll do it wrong! So pruning in a 'HEAD garden' has 3 easy to follow steps.

If in doubt don't – there may be times when you need to watch aspects of the garden or your own growth more closely. If you think there might be goodness there, leave it alone and don't be in so much of a hurry to get a result. Go round another cycle and see what time brings!

Measure twice cut once! Although often a woodwork expression, it works here because you need to look carefully and don't snip off potential because you didn't see it at first glance.

Cut cleanly. If you are going to 'cut' off a department, team or function, do so cleanly, clearly and don't leave raggy edges! A solid change policy and process is one thing, but ensuring people understand why the pruning is happening, where, when and for whom will go much further than surprise and inequitable removals with no apparent rhyme or reason.

Afterthought:

If there is a storm / bad weather approaching your business, do not use that as an excuse to prune but rather focus on how to protect your business and your people from it – what can we do together not who can I get rid of to ride the bad times. Slash and burn is not pruning it is simple destruction – and you can be sure those who see it or who are damaged by it wont be around next year to help you grow even stronger than you are now!

PART 2

Tools and Techniques for Results

Different Types of Gardens

TOOLS AND TECHNIQUES FOR RESULTS

Here's a little list of tools you might like to think about when you are applying the model of HEAD Gardening in your life!

Tool	HEAD Gardener Usage
Fork	For digging into / up a plant without damaging its roots – perhaps lifting a person out from a team without disturbing the good work of others – also creates the space for them to move into the gap!
Spade	Bigger rooted plants or people to be dug up and make a big change. Also used to dig over the soil, aerate it and shake up the environment.
Trowel	Smaller than a spade but able to dig into an environment and create a space to plant something or someone new amongst others.
Soil sifter	A refining of the environment to sift out stones or that which is surplus to requirement and only focus on the good, fine environment for growth.
Secateurs	For careful pruning, snipping off of small aspects of an otherwise well developing plant. Used for taking out unhelpful spurs of activity when the energy needs to be focussed the growth of the main plant. Keeps the edges of people and plants tidy!
Rake	Can either be used to softly cover new seeds with soil to assist in their growth, like induction support and onboarding, or, for efficiently drawing together old dried leaves, grass or 'gone over' excess to go onto the compost heap.

Plant pot	A job. Each job has a role, with boundaries and expectations of what will be achieved within it. Comes in different sizes and should grow in size as the plant or person grows.
Watering can	Provides mandatory support and development.
Gloves	Protects the gardener when tackling thorny issues or stingers! Perhaps use like a policy – followed and interpreted to the specific conditions of use.
Kneelers	When getting into the 'nitty gritty' helps provide comfort and resilience to stay there a bit longer and really get the work done.
Loppers	For more substantial issues, bigger action is sometimes needed, and to let in 'light' removing old branches can be very beneficial.
Wheelbarrow	Carries goodness to where you need it and takes away the unneeded. Like excellent admin, vital to support you in your garden, and whose use is often undersung!
Garden hose	To water those often unseen (or unheard) parts of the garden. Walk to the edges and listen to all and add water (see petal 7) where needed.
Saw	Even more substantial than loppers. Where organisations need to stop doing something, remove a product line, close a department, a strong clear tool is needed which will be effective and clean.
Shed	Where we go to reflect, clean our tools, take a nap, look for pieces of string and potter about. A gardeners safe space.

Technique 1 – Weeding and Pest Management

One of my favourite activities in the garden is weeding. It takes out all the 'bad' from where I don't want it, and I can turn it into 'good' by adding it to the compost heap. A very fulfilling activity.

But what is a weed really? To Cecelia Ahern a weed is *'a flower growing in the wrong place'* and to Ralph Waldo Emerson *'a plant whose virtues have not yet been discovered'*. And its true, to some extent, some plants have a lot to offer, even if you don't want them in your border! But others… are pernicious, poisonous, sneaky, and downright dangerous. Both types, are much like people.

I am sure I am not alone to a feeling I have had where I was doing my best to fit in and be 'corporate' in a professional setting, but something wasn't sitting quite right? Looking around me and thinking how superior others believe themselves to be, or the vast gap between their world and mine? Or even thinking, no, it's not me, it is YOU! So, I do know what it's like to be considered a 'weed' and yet also to be trying my best to join in, flower at the right time, use the nutrients and water and seek to thrive. Only for some 'gardener' type to come along, dig me up and chuck me away. No thought to how I felt about it, or what they were missing but just a blinkered view of the world – or border – that had to be as it had to be, and that there was no suggestion of replanting me elsewhere in the garden, or considering if I might have other worth? Nope, just up and chuck.

The good news is that the border wasn't actually very healthy anyway, the other plants not cared for, and to be honest, was going to wither away anyway if there wasn't a radical replan. But I was composted, and all to the good, for after a while, I was able to use that learning in fertilizing others, as a nutrient to help others grow in my next role.

Are you familiar with that story? One where you are not being nurtured or are you not nurturing others who you consider to be weeds? Why is that so?

What is it about them that you want to dig up and is spoiling your garden?

What is it about them that is not fitting in with your vision of the garden that you had?

And are they 'transferable' even convertible to be allowed to thrive in your plan?

Perhaps not, but then you need to have the conversation that explains that, take responsibility for your vision, and how they do not fit in with that which you are seeking to create.

In most instances and industries, we call these conversations 'performance management', but remember, as the leader of this person (or weed!) you are also responsible in part for their performance, ability, clarity and confidence to be competent.

Have you <u>really</u> done what you needed to do before deciding to dig them out?

Do they even know they are not doing as you hoped? Intended? Or required?

There are indeed some weeds for whom only the deep chemicals (or preferably soap, salt and vinegar as an organic version!) are needed to obliterate them. These weeds are not really people but behaviours. We hear of 'toxic cultures' and poor behaviour going unchallenged, some even ending up in legal cases and employment tribunals. These types of weeds are the ones like poisoned ivy, get everywhere, have immensely strong and deep roots, suffocate and strangle everything in its path, suck the life and nutrients from others and keep climbing higher and higher to the light.

We know these people. We know who they are and often they know who they are, but don't care. So, what are you going to do about these weeds?

Well, we can hand pick them out, one by one, but the world shows us that even if you topple one dictator or toxic leader there is always another just waiting in the wings (or may even be offering to pluck out the original weed!!!). We have two other basic options. One is to try and turn over the soil and sift the weeds out that way – that way you tackle and remove the offending behaviour, person, or influence through the management of role changes and structures. Secondly, you can take radical action and either smother them and remove all light and chance of water using a method of exclusion – black plastic layers in gardens, but I think this is as bad as the behaviours in the first place! So if you can, find a louder voice or voices of champions for good qualities, to show in stark relief the benefit of the goodness you seek for your team, and the weed will either turn and join this joyful, fruitful, productive team or will more likely go elsewhere, and that's ok too. It takes all sorts to make a world.

Alternatively, just leave them where they are and invite those who enjoy that environment to work with it. The 'do nothing' option is still a choice and an action in its own right.

Advantages to having weeds in your team?

Actually, yes!

In a garden, predators, insects often feed off the 'flowery weeds' and go on and eat the aphids that spoil our roses and vegetables. So for us humans, we can learn that there are some tasks these 'not initially desired' team members can have which others may not wish to do, but that they love, and it's the getting the balance right that matters here so we do not indulge too much errant behaviour but allow for difference to bring challenge and their own contribution which is different from our own.

If weeds are growing in a garden, then you know the soil is good for growing, and in a team, well there is energy and life in there which might not be directed in the right way but there is certainly something to work with rather than a barren landscape!

Weeds can be turned into compost as I have said, and it helps others to learn from the lessons of the past by having this cycle of that learning ploughed back into the team to help them grow from lessons learnt.

Pest management

The difference between a pest and a weed is that a pest is an animal, and it is eating the wrong things, and by that, I mean, eating the plants and achievements you are seeking rather than something else! Your garden is a veritable smorgasbord of delicious delights and tasty morsels so that the abundance of your brilliance is indeed very attractive to those in need (or greed!). As a living creature all animals have a right to eat and be, but to avoid all your hard work going to feed a family of mice or insects or even perhaps all of your salads now devoured by slugs and snails, you can take some precautions. And I would advise that you do!

In your office, you will no doubt have intellectual property policies, data protection processes and procedures and all the expected governance that you should do for even owning a garden – or business – never mind dealing with the pests. So for pest management we try and stick to 5 basic rules;

- **Make something else more attractive** than spoiling your work (by eating it!)

- **Keep the maintenance and 'pruning' up to date** so you know where there is badness beginning to grow or be a haven for pests

- **Investing in your people** (plants) and teams means that the odd 'nibble' from a roving pest will hardly be noticed as they will be strong enough to fight them off!

- **Net young growth**, by which I mean, only allow to connect with the more vulnerable those you can trust to work with them and teach them well so they have a fighting chance – like netting Kale to keen safe from the white butterflies who lay their eggs on them and the caterpillars then eat it!

- **Make it clear that pests will not be tolerated** and that there is a procedure to deal with them which will be followed! Be that disciplinary or financially punitive.

Tecnique 2 – Creating colour that lasts (Talent management / retention)

When you plant a seed, you don't turn up the next morning and expect to see a beautiful flower. You know by now you need a plan and a few actions, including patience.

For our people, and I am including all people here, be that in the professional environment or not, the development of beauty, strength, even nutrition through produce comes through the management of that talent with the aim of retaining that person to become a force for good in the team, the business, and then to grow into leading parts of it, as they – or you! – become more experienced and able.

So how can we create colour that lasts in our people, ensuring they are energised, well, and continue in their efforts for a successful team or business?

There is so much written about talent management and retention that I wonder if that is indeed the problem. We can describe it, create programmes for it, even commentate on how others should be doing it better, but really isn't it about being a human helping other humans achieve their goals and then encouraging more and further purpose and opportunities?

When your Sweet Peas (and Cosmos for that matter) flower, they 'enjoy' being picked because it stimulates others to growth. If left on the stem, they have their day, and then turn into a seed pod, and others are not encouraged to flourish.

For leaders – or HEAD Gardeners – the focus needs to be the creating of the conditions, and then the noticing and encouraging by whatever suitable method works, for the talent around you. Its also important to realise that while some talents are a perfect fit for an organisation or team, some are not – or the organisation is not ready for them.

It doesn't make the person less talented; it is that the environment cannot support their growth – so they need to either go to another part of the same garden or find a new one. That's not a bad thing, that is creating colour that lasts and doesn't have a quick flash of brilliance and then be forgotten about.

The other challenge to give some thought to is, why are you creating the colour that lasts? Do you really want that? Or is your business a fast-moving ever-changing garden which needs people coming and going to keep it fresh? Perhaps sometimes you want to draw the eye to colour in one part of the garden and then as soon as it has fulfilled its purpose move the attention to another part, and for the people or produce in the first aspect to rest and regenerate – or be annuals in any case so are 'one and done'. That's ok if you collected the seeds of their learning and choose to plant them somewhere else next or for another purpose. So there is a choice about retention here not just an expectation that it is a good thing. Many businesses will say 'ah yes but recruitment is expensive, and we need to keep costs down', ok, so why not create groups who work together and can cycle through different time and roles and aspects of working on projects or change programmes where it is appropriate to have a high turnover rather than a carte blanche approach to the whole organisation?

Go back to the garden. There is no 'one plant everywhere' approach in any garden, even if there are varieties of the same, such as stunning azalea or rhododendron gardens (like Exbury in the South of England) there is still room for others too, and the art is to create the evolving nature of the garden not to have one static display and be 'finished'. Gardens are never 'finished' and neither are people until they pass back to the earth – and even then their essence and legacies often live on in others and other manifestations. So creating colour that lasts is a concept that has practical applications and uses the building blocks of talent management but is a different perspective to achieve a more sustainable and sustaining outcome for all.

Technique 3 – Seasonal planting (Career management)

'To everything there is a season' it says in The Bible (Ecclesiastes 3) *'a time to plant and a time to pluck up what has been planted'* and this is true of our careers and lives too. In our temperate climates North and South hemispheres have 4 seasons, as we recognise in our lives and much literature; poems such as Pied Beauty (Gerard Manley Hopkins) for Autumn, or in the book, film and play The Great Gatsby where it starts in the Spring and as the tension increases it moves to the suffocating heat of Summer. We have used seasons as metaphor in literature for the birth of life in Spring, the Summer salad days, the Autumn of reflection, harvest and older age and then Winter when all dies back. Yet this is not true across the whole world, and in places nearer the equator there are two key seasons: the wet and the dry. Here, there is much movement of life to achieve the necessary input to maintain it.

Here in the UK, we have been used to the 4 seasons, and although our climate is changing, we are continuing to map our planting and rotation of plants within these 4 seasons, even if we are now looking to take account of the changing temperatures, water and therefore soil and environment impact, to the extent that some gardens are now considering how to introduce plants that will survive in the driest of conditions which we are unaccustomed to.

This survival and flexibility, adaptation to the seasons and the need to take account of our environment is entirely true of our personal and team career management too. It would be more than a little unwise to expect a new team leader to deliver success and a positive team cohesion and results without paying a little attention to the environment around them.

We, as individuals, can take account of what we are 'ready' for, and what we will do in the cycle of arriving in a new role, developing new skills – be they technical knowledge or leadership style. Then we begin to get into our stride and more comfortable with the role, and then as we mature our career bears fruit, and it is in the stepping back, and Winter of our professional lives, that we might consider what we can or could do differently or more/less off were it Spring again. As Percy Byshe Shelley wrote in Ode to the West Wind *"If Winters here can Spring be far behind"* and we could do well to remember this in the Winter of professional moments. We may have another version of ourselves to come!

Another trait of a gardener is to be resilient and patient when things go wrong and the unexpected comes and destroys good plants. For example, an early or late frost might cause damage or destruction to young shoots in the Spring, and although it is also the responsibility of a gardener to look after these young and vulnerable plants, there are times when that simply cannot or does not happen.

How do we deal with that in our lives then? Our leaders should be able to see many storms coming or snaps of frost that will damage us, so what are our mechanisms for protecting our business? It will be different for each but in principle the same, 'prepare for the worst and hope for the best'. It is a foolish leader who imagines that they have control over everything. That praxis of resilience with a team and group of people has been trained for over generations and in business as much as the military or becoming an astronaut! Each of us need to prepare for our seasons as an individual, and then work together as teams to be strong, with the organisational vision to be the guiding light to lead us through the tough times. Voltaire ends his work Candide with the phrase *"We must cultivate our own garden"* suggesting a moral that that if we all looked after our own lives before telling others how to look after theirs the world would be a better place. More commonly now we use the airline safety briefing 'always put on your own mask before helping others with theirs', but it means the same thing.

– 4 –

DIFFERENT TYPES OF GARDEN

1 – The productive gardener – getting more!

If I have read one book or learnt and used one model on increasing productivity, I have read hundreds. Truly. We use the word in every industry and sector as if just by saying it there is a magical formula that somehow will make the world a better place. What we really mean however, is either

- getting more with what we have or
- doing the same for less cost or
- doing / getting more for less effort or cost.

In a private enterprise it is usually to seek the very last of these, getting more for giving less, the P&L demands it and business needs to grow or is overtaken by others, so why not squeeze the fruit til the last drop of juice comes out, and then squeeze a little more just in case before you discard it.

The public sector has a similar, but perhaps less ruthless approach – maybe not, that's another book! – but certainly the use of the taxpayer dollar / pound is something that has a different accountability to it as the tax payer has a level of control over the 'give and the gets' for the financial investment. I say some level of control because we know there are always choices in how taxes are spent, the needs and wants always outstrip supply, so those in Government, of whatever flavour or country it represents must choose between education, bin collection, health provision and security of their nation, to name but a few priorities.

So, in the garden, how do you get more with less? Or more with the same? And as in life, there are some aspects to this which are entirely applicable to our own and our teams and organisations productivity.

One of the key aspects is timing. I have a love of growing tomatoes – not just because of their goodness, taste, colour, flexibility of use, but because for every single tomato they contain tens and hundreds of seeds for the next years tomatoes. I once took tomatoes of a particularly sweet little cherry tomato variety (Gardeners Delight if you must know!) and have had a whole season the following year of tomatoes. That is certainly productive, and I could then take the fruit from the bountiful and ongoing harvest in the same way year after year, and still am.

It goes like this: *I took 3 tomatoes, carefully deseeded them in about July/August, dried the seeds on kitchen paper, put them in an envelope once dried, and got them out in February, planted each one in an old toilet paper tube with some soil and kept them inside until they showed shoots, grew them on, pinched out the flowers as they were in early growth (so they direct more energy to the roots / no blossom end rot and so on) then snipped off more leafy suckers beneath the first proper flowers for fruit as they are not 'worth the candle' (i.e. won't create fruit) and slow down real fruit development, and then potted them on until I ended up with plants I couldn't reach the top of and needed steps to collect the juicy tomatoes.* One of my first videos about being The HEAD Gardener was about tomatoes so have a look if your interested!

Firstly, you can see the small investment of actual product to give me a bigger return on my investment. The production speaks for itself. But more than that, the time, effort, care, interest, nuture, consistency and dedication I have given to this plant is the thing that makes the difference.

The measurements of physical capital, technology, human capital (labour) and natural resources are exactly the same for growing the tomatoes in a garden as they are for increasing the outputs and getting a better return on investment for a business.

Sure, there are books written on the habits of highly effective people (thank you Stephen Covey for his *'7 habits'*), even *'Extreme Productivity' 'Atomic Habits'* (love that!) *'80/20'* and even in coaching for high performance it is rare not to touch on productivity somewhere in the conversation. The key thing about the productive HEAD garden is that within all the inputs for outputs are the words and actions that give **consistency, care and patience** in order to gain the truly productive outputs, outcomes, and critically, sustain them.

The environment you provide, the culture you create and the leadership you show, is what will make the difference between a productive garden in your team or not. Did you know that the most common problem with tomatoes is black spot? (Back to tomatoes!)

And the only reason it happens is because of the inconsistency in watering? You see, the garden has the answers. Its nature looking at us wondering why we are not following its lessons, and we in turn wonder how we can tame it to our will and joy!

And it's funny, when you think about the environment you provide your people and seek to create a productive one. The gardener doesn't turn up in the morning to the garden and shout at it to grow quicker? That would be ridiculous – in fact people who shout at people at work are. Yes. I called it out. Ridiculous! It shows a lack of control not power or might. So, no shouting at the plants! Its only for danger warnings in an emergency. But in an office? Never. So, the gardener looks at the health of the plants, sees what more he/she/they can do to support the growth, and through that focus productivity is inspired, not created. The innovation that these elements bring are what enables the space to think, the ideas to flow and the new more efficient and effective ways of operating to emerge.

To have a productive HEAD garden, yes, you need a tidy, weed free, well organised plan and intention. Then add some good quality ingredients / resources / seedlings call them what you will, and then, then LOOK AFTER THEM. As Richard Branson said *look after your people and your people will look after your business.* I believe he was right.

2 – The sensory garden – related to behaviours.

Have you ever been to a sensory garden? I think I have seen and enjoyed them in parts of other gardens, but I am not sure I could manage a whole garden setting off all my senses in one go! I am one of those – I think lucky – ones who has something called synaesthesia and it is a gift but I think I might get overload if all my senses were set off at once! I hear music and see colours; I hear words and see shapes, I saw a painting once which had a very distinctive 'smell', days of the week have colours! So you might have to bear with me here, because to me the concept of the sensory garden is one I have enjoyed (although can be exhausting), and one I find useful, when thinking of HEAD gardening – partly because it is natural, but partly because I can see how so many of our behaviours are aligned to our senses. I'll show you what I mean. As beginners, we will start at the beginning.

A sensory garden is named such as it is supposed to stimulate the senses of sight, smell, hearing, taste (sometimes) and touch. I wonder if that's all gardens. Surely? With emphasis on one or more than another sense. But there are also literary gardens (Shakespeare Garden at Herstmonceux Castle) or water lily gardens (Claude Monet's inspiration) and when you see any garden it stimulates any one or more of our senses.

The scent of jasmine garden I mentioned earlier, box hedges that are fun to pat as they are soft and bouncy, and I once had a bamboo garden which rustled in the breeze as I sat there of an evening. All this sounds very good for us, and it is, but it is also a human reaction to a stimulus, which, like the way we interact with other people can be inspiring, joyful, growthful or conversely, very much, not.

I see the senses that gardens stimulate and the behaviours we can role model and use as a force for good as follows:

Sight – looking at someone when you speak to them is an acknowledgement of their and your attention to the conversation. In some cultures looking directly at someone can cause offence, and for the differently abled and sight impaired this is not possible. However, for the focus of this book I am talking about acknowledging the existence of another person, to create a respect and connection between people to know there is an equity in that relationship as human beings through that behaviour. People who suffer from a lack of confidence often struggle with this one, but it is one of the most vital and connective ways of communicating with another human, to look at them as they speak and when you speak. I believe that respect comes from the very basic acknowledgment of existence, and for that, we need to look and see, then absorb and process.

Sound – this relates to the phrase 'understand before being understood'. To 'listen with fascination' as Professor Michael West would say. And truly listen. Not only to what is being said but to the tone, the pace, the pain or pleasure in the sharing, the emotion and need through the sounds.

Taste – Some days we like sweet or savoury dishes or treats, and I see this sense as one which is about tuning in your behaviour to others and noticing others with theirs. Its not about 'fitting in' it's a sense of 'is this a bright bunch of flowers moment?' Smiley, joyful, bright perhaps? Or is it a chilli pepper type moment? With a bit of a kick and a bit of 'pow zap wahay!' You get the idea. This is about ensuring there are no clashes in your garden. Difference yes, clashes no.

Smell – this is one of the most evocative for me. On the one hand we have heard of the 'smell of success' in business but also hear of 'something doesn't smell quite right' and some people even talk about the 'smell of the rain' (which is an actual chemical release and moistening in the ground from plants as the rain begins to fall!) The smell we usually have in our sensory garden is most commonly to bring pleasure. Where we can squeeze a mint leaf to bring a fresh 'zap' to our senses, or a lavender crushed gives a relaxing response, it is for us in our HEAD gardens to consider the smell we want to leave with someone.

A very old wizened tiny and self-contained man of Asian heritage I used know asked me once what 'fragrance I wanted to leave behind' as my legacy. It was a curious question but one I have never forgotten, and it is one which I subsequently found out is anchored in a letter from a Christian man called Paul to the Corinthians where he wrote about the 'scent' that he and his other followers left behind was 'the sweet aroma of the knowledge of Him' meaning Christ.

It has always stayed with me about the 'scent' that I leave behind, not in a literal way but the impression I leave on people, and I think its one for ongoing reflection. What is the scent that you leave behind? Energising? Inspiring? Memorable? Have a think.

Touch – Finally this sense is closely related to sight really. This is about how we might feel if touched. Sometimes we are prickly, sometimes soft, or tight, taut, coiled spring, tender, gentle, wired, springy, tigger-like, flat, deflated, dried up, soggy, lethargic, you will have your own words….

The touch refers to the behaviour that is the mood you choose to bring into a room or into a garden. You can decide – sometimes harder than others, and sometimes a great personal effort, how you are showing up, and I deliberately wanted to ensure we had a focus on this aspect of behaviour because as Victor Frankl was famous for saying *"Everything can be taken from a man* but one thing: the last of the human freedoms – to choose one's attitude in any given set of circumstances to choose one's own way"* (*or other gender identity).

So how we choose to show up to others, and how we would 'feel' is someone described touching us is a very important aspect of our behaviour.

- How would you feel if someone 'touched' you right now?

- Describe the last person you communicated with using the language of touch.

If it's hard to do, maybe do it the other way around? Think of someone who has spikey leaves? Or perhaps a delicate flower? This is using the creative aspect of the brain to think about something or someone you know in a different way.

3 – The mature garden

Keeping going

When a garden matures it can become one of two things, possibly at the same time, either becoming comfortable and undemanding in its own self, and settling into growing gently and slowly, able to weather any storms, has seen it all before, and knows that this too will pass. And / or it becomes a little bit of a 'grande dame' and can be a puffed with its own self importance and experience. The first has a charm, the latter sometimes commands respect but is less attractive, even if there is something to learn from it, it can squash the smaller plants trying to find their way and steal light as they fear their grandeur and place in the garden will fade all too soon and they will be dug up or chopped down.

To continue a mature garden – or let's be honest, a mature head in the garden – takes the balance of using the experience and ability to cope with feast or famine, scorching sun drying out roots or sitting getting their roots wet for week after week. A mature garden gives stability, brings a peace in achievement already gained and offers the picture of what others can aspire to.

Some mature gardens/gardeners choose (either willingly or through circumstance) to ease back a bit on growth at this time, looking back on their journey and that which they have produced for others, shaded others from and are a reflective space which gives them a sense of 'it is enough just to be now'. Others however have a lot more to offer! They might want to share cuttings, grow new parts of themselves or find a lease of life due to new energy, soil or plants, joining them in their border, or a new skill – more people than plant! – to engage in and to begin to grow in new ways. They may leave this garden and have their roots split and leave one legacy here and go and start growing again somewhere else. New environments new challenges new adventures. And why not? This is where a mature garden can take its strength to new places and bring joy and learning to new audiences.

Do you have any mature gardens in your organisation? How do you honour them? All they see and have endured, share and have experienced? Listen to their stories and grow from their experiences – good and bad.

4 – Reviving an old garden.

I am sure we have all heard of gardens being 'lost' or 'found' and certainly in many domestic houses where the owner has either not had the interest or ability so the garden becomes overgrown over time. The brambles grow, suffocate the delicate plants and the beauty of previously cared for plants and people. One of the famous 'lost' gardens in England are the Lost Gardens of Heligan, in which 200 acres of garden simply grew over and were forgotten since World War 1 and on rediscovery in 1990 became Europe's biggest ever garden restoration project. These gardens are now visited and enjoyed by hundred and thousands of us ever year. Here, in the rediscovery they learned about new ways of creating gardens, harnessing old methods and continuing the evolution.

Lynne Copp, Founder of the *Worklife Company*, is one of the leading lights in the exploration of what she calls the '3rd 3rd', which is the third part of our life, after growing up and parenting perhaps, then working and growing to a maturity in the second phase, when the third part arrives there are many, women in particular, who are now seeking to create something for themselves, their lives, their HEAD gardens or actual businesses!

In conversation with Lynne, she talks about the re-finding of parts of ourselves, almost like coming round the corner into a whole new garden 'room' and saying 'ah! I know this! I remember this! I was good at this!' whatever that skill maybe. Or uncovering and remembering how good the ground was, could be again, and the skill and knowledge not used for a while can be nurtured back to strength and on to create opportunity, joy and achievement for the third part of life.

She says *"I want women to recognise that during the final 3rd of their life, that we can work together to make a difference, build a community of wisdom, and make a significant difference to each woman and man living in the previous thirds, in all environments, and across our world. Now that is a track that I for one would love to look back down at the end of my own final 3rd."*

I have a feeling that this resonates for most in that season of life, and indeed removes a fear for those for whom it is to come. Whilst not a garden per se, I notice the words 'environment' and 'a track' to look back down, and see in Lynne's words that however we describe the contribution we make there is a real ease in connection with the natural (nature itself) and then the cultivated (the garden) where the rhythms and knowledge seem to be inherent to us.

The joy in considering the revival of an old garden is that we know there is a wealth of experience and gems to be discovered again and all can access and learn from that uncovering to create the gardens next identity and an excitement in that unknown.

5 – What type of garden am I?

So how do you know what conditions suit you? And how can you grow your best HEAD garden?

The short answer to the first question is honestly, it doesn't matter. The fact is that you are a living being and seek to exist and thrive (not survive) where you can grow. Humans do as well as our plants do – usually for most of their lives – wherever they find themselves. However, if you want to thrive, and choose as azaleas and rhododendrons do to thrive in acid soil or lavender in alkaline, then you will need to make some deliberate decisions.

You start with Petal 1 and work your way through the model with an outcome in mind. The purpose of using the garden as an analogy is to connect us with other living and thriving (or not) parts of the world that need tending and supporting as we do. Some people like the cut and thrust of work and success like an arid cactus garden, some are more a formal structured and bounded garden. There are others, my friend the late Professor Aidan Halligan for example, who one might describe as a wildflower meadow – entirely uncontainable but utterly full of beautiful colours, special flowers which self-seed, and who saw life as a joyful opportunity to be grasped.

And there are those of us complex beings who are many different sorts of garden all at the same time. We like our productive garden which strives to deliver the highest quality and quantity of fruit and vegetables to sustain others, we want a cutting garden of flowers to bring into the house and home and give to others. We want carpets of primroses in Spring, the scent of lavender and roses, big blousy peonies and quiet fritillaries nestling in the grass as Spring becomes high Summer, watching Acers burst into flame in their reds and oranges of Autumn as the pumpkins arrive and then spiky, red-berried holly, and snow drops in the Winter.

As people we are not one type of garden, we are all that nature is. From lily pond to rock garden, from highly manicured lawn or terracing to gardens based on themes – literary, artist palette, or chefs garden we can choose to be one kind of garden, and gardener or another. And in our quests, we can learn and grow and become a different type of garden at different times of our life. Share cuttings, take seeds, explore ideas as you garden through life, and the success you cultivate will be as special and unique as every garden you see about you from the functional and perhaps ordinary to the vastly ornate and visited. We come from the earth, and you can shape it as well as it is shaping you. Now you have some knowledge, a new perspective, a way of thinking and acting, perhaps you might like to try to take action – perhaps for the thousandth time? But this time, I walk with you, the tools and skills of this Beginners Guide can be your prop, your 'go to' where no question is too stupid, no worry to small to share or think through how to dissolve it into something more manageable, and where your hard work, patience and creativity will bring you the answers you need to cultivate your success whatever it that means for you.

PART 3

Cultivating Success in our World

Part 3 comprises of 4 short essays to support leadership in cultivating success, in a sustainable, real and outcome focussed way. It looks at the task of 'growing people' to achieve their goals and beyond through the lens of all that must be harnessed and contended with. The world of 2023 is a far cry from 1973 and will be from 2073, so from half a century of learning come some suggestions for action for the next.

CULTIVATING SUCCESS IN OUR WORLD

OUR ENVIRONMENT THROUGH THE WORLD LENS

When we take a step back from the 'ploughing of our own furrow' of focussed delivery, or searching for purpose, and look at the world 'out there', we can see the global picture is one of complexity, concern and strife to say the least. We have the crises of war, tearing up peoples lives and opportunities to grow and spread economic and relationship joy and success. We see the damage we humans are doing to the very place we call home – be it from geographical wars or wars on the world itself as we damage the very planet we live on. We feel the pinch of an economic, and cost of living, crisis, where the price of everything is going up and our ability to achieve such gains is going down. A bleak outlook.

However, as Edmund Burke (may have) said *"The only thing necessary for the triumph of evil is that good men do nothing".* And it is this lens that I want us to explore what we CAN do, what we can cultivate and how each of us can contribute, as HEAD gardeners ourselves, to make progress toward a better tomorrow.

As I have said before, gardeners are optimists, they have to be! And it is also needed for those taking action to lead a part of our world as a corporate, multi-national or small to medium size enterprise. I am not suggesting that we all go gardening or as one of my former Directors said 'don't landscape your garden when your house is on fire' but I am suggesting that we look at the traits and actions of gardeners to help us live more peaceably now and cultivate that better outcome for the future – financial, economic, relational and physical.

From a snippet of a radio programme I heard on BBC Radio 4 talking about potential, there was, at the top of the programme a voice sharing how potential is a seed, which can either be watered and grow, or left to the side in a dark room and will not. From all that you have read already in the Beginners Guide you know that growing people is all about that. And my premise here is that potential, combined with opportunity and hard work cultivates success.

Potential x Opportunity x Work = Success

We – globally and individually – have choices to make. Do we have the potential to save the world from so damaging itself?

Yes, we understand the problems, we have control (in the main) of our own choices and influence over others, as well as not over dwelling on action we have neither control nor influence.

We can – another choice – support and help ourselves and others in creating opportunities for fulfilling that potential.

Finally, we have the agency to choose how hard we work. Sometimes we are limited by factors beyond our control its true, perhaps our health or other responsibilities limit how much we can work even if we would like to do more.

I go back to the equation. For each element has a value and a focus. Each element can be great or small, but without one of the triumvirate in the equation success is not the outcome. Failure, dissatisfaction, disappointment, damage, can be the flip side of our success coin, where lack of potential, lack of opportunity and lack of effort are all going to lead to failure. This is where thinking 'bigger' comes in. Set your mind into the 'grand strategic' space.

The insult of the successful not wishing to entertain 'hard luck' stories, are just that, an insult. There will always be people for whom great office, power, and success is expected, but that does not mean that the 'have nots' in opportunity terms do not have exactly the same, or more, potential, it is that the opportunities are not offered or obvious. Nor is the knowledge to know that work is required. How can we expect anyone to flourish, blossom, share their seeds of success with that start?

My recommendation, therefore, is that for all we do in a self-growth focus, we need to put the same or more effort into others. We might find ourselves being even more successful than we even imagined then! I did not come down in the last shower, and I know there are people for whom self-aggrandizement and power, money and being seen as a success their own version of living a good life and will do their bit when they can afford to. But my view is that this is what got us into this mess of economic, cultural, relational and destruction of our world.

Perhaps just reading this is the catalyst you need to do more, say more, give more, share more. Perhaps you think you do your bit already. Maybe you do. Yet we know, gardens take ongoing maintenance, attention, patience and care… and so does our world. Perhaps you might look again? Just in case there is a seed of potential or an opportunity you have missed? Or a bit more, or different, work you or your organisation can do to improve the garden of the world. It would be a shame to be the one who missed it and the world continued to suffer because you didn't make that choice.

LEADING THE WORKFORCE TODAY, TOMORROW AND BEYOND

I want to stop off here on the subject of leadership through HEAD Gardening as the world of work and the future of that work continues to change.

We know from research stretching back before the concept of people development even began that there will always be change and evolution, and sometimes revolution which will change the way we work, the work we do, where and how we do it, and how and who does it. With all these variables how can a leader today lead and grow their people in a meaningful sustaining way for delivery today but readiness for tomorrow? Maybe they can't? Would that be ok if it were so?

We all know the spectrum of learning from yesterday, delivering today and shaping or be shaped by tomorrow. For example, the UK has a multi-billion-pound health service, based on annual budget and business cycles, and yet also combine this short-termism with a 10-year plan and vision. Add to those aspects of multi-decade investments in areas such as diagnostic services and new hospitals. There are many 'lines of development' on differing timescales, all running at the same time. The same is true for other public services in care, education, defence, emergency services and so on.

The for-profit sector has more room to manoeuvre and perhaps a clearer picture, from my experience, around the short, medium and longer-term horizons. There are choices to be made around making money today, tomorrow and in the long term, and the benefits or disbenefits of each, given the mega trends across the long term, the clarity and prioritisation of the multi-year customer/geographical segments while considering the innovation roadmap. And of course there is the short term, quick buck, execution and creativity in delivering 'jam today' whilst not damaging the medium or long term.

What kind of leader does all that need (either public or private bodies) where the clarity goes from gin clear 8/8th blue to smog?

I posture that it is a HEAD Gardener Leader that follows the laws and joys of nature and gardening that will be most successful. Even if the produce your organisation delivers is a 'widget' of some kind, you will not be the only person in that organisation. There will be others who can help or hinder its success. Therefore, they need to be motivated, supported, understand the requirement and grow – often beyond their own imaginings.

A leader in the work of the future needs to;

- be aware of the big 'climate changes' in their industry, acknowledge the megatrends of new or lost parts of their garden,

- distract the aphids from the succulent new shoots by being the colourful marigold to draw the attention away from damaging the people,

- provide a canopy of shelter when needed, but not become a 'legend in their own lunchtime' so the story is 'all about me'.

For me it appears that there are two core parts of leading in the future of the work we all do. The first is looking after the growing others, the second is growing self. These two parts are as important as each other.

Without investing in growing self and becoming both aware and accepting of the future of the world of work, the leader will loose touch with the workforce and try to instil an old way into a new generation who have already moved on. I am not saying that there isn't some value in experience, even that which comes from 'we did this before' but it is exceptionally important to ensure that the conditions are the same if you think you are doing the same thing again, because if you're not, how do you know you are going to get the same answer?

Being open to others new ways of achieving better outcomes, productivity, happier staff or self may not be an indicator you are 'doing it wrong' but is worth exploring how to do it 'more right'. The self-growth is not being selfish or self-indulgent, it is in service of your garden, your people. They need to know this, so tell them. That's ok. An executive that disappears off for a new experience or immersion in another environment may be pillaried by the workforce if they don't understand the purpose, how it will be used for their benefit, and perhaps even seen simply as a 'jolly' while the rest of the workforce works. As with our traditional control circles, the leader can only control own behaviour, influence others, and there is a world out there you have neither impact on. Therefore, the biggest mistake is to imagine that because you have told someone – the workforce – about your investment in you, that they have heard or understood. Your authenticity in sharing your explorations and experience and learning will be a good start, but the proof will be in the changes in your behaviour, the use of new knowledge to help them grow differently – more easily perhaps, with a new frame of reference or a more relevant, new model, method or process.

One health warning to this leader-learning and then sharing comes from my days working with a group of military personnel who taught me the phrase a 'CORGI'. This is a Commanding Officers Really Good Idea. I am sure you realise it is clearly thought of as anything but! I imagine you can understand the look that goes with the sentence "Is this something that will really make a difference or is it a CORGI? We often get these after

'X' has been to a conference…". Therefore, a word to the wise here. Test your 'brilliant' new idea and learning for your growth with a few trusted folks and critical friends before launching it to the world!

Turning to the growth of people and their experiences and outputs at work, the second key role of leader. There are thousands if not millions of ways to lead your people well (and badly!) and a matching number of theories, models, methods and even analogies.

My key offering is to **underpin every conversation and action by attaching it to the purpose of the business and values which drive the outcome.**

If you can't make a direct link, don't spend any more time on it. If it is health, then the purpose is the best experience and outcome possible for patient and staff member. Why would you do anything that does not lead to that? For NASA it was 'put a man on the moon' in 1961. So what is your real purpose? Perhaps have a think through the vision of Petal 1 of the HEAD Gardener model to be sure and go from there!

TECHNOLOGY GROWTH AND PEOPLE GROWTH

One of the very core reasons for the development of the HEAD Gardener is that as the world of technology, digital, automation, cyber grow in our world – and enable, enhance, and improve our lives in many beneficial ways, it occurred to me that we need to pay as much or more attention to the growth of our people as well as our 'tech'.

As with much of the theme of the Beginners Guide there is a core of balance required to ensure both progress and contentment in the 'garden'. The focus on HEAD Gardening therefore supports the new frontiers and wider possibilities that our technological innovations afford.

Our plants need sunshine and showers, our human lives need activity and sleep, and our heads function at their optimum when they are nurtured and supported as well as stretched and challenged by new ways of working or possibilities.

My version of considering the balance of technology growth and people growth is to ensure that this is based on a few principles. You can choose how you execute them, but I will give you some examples.

For those in the deep tech world, there their profession is immersed in innovation and creation, exploration and new abilities they – as a general sweeping statement – might find the most difference and/or difficulty in interacting with those from the non-tech human world. The gulf between the way people think and behave and the deep understanding of coding or cyber security, process automation or digital invention take two different types of thinking, and ability. The irony being that we begin to understand this through the good offices of science, technology and being able to

115

interpret brain activity patterns, which in themselves are borne out of technological enablement. We have come a long way in understanding the spectrum of neurodiversity and how the 'wiring' of our brains can differ immensely from one human to another. However different we are from one another we do all need the basics – light, sleep, nutrition, stimulation to a greater or lesser extent and to be able to interact with other humans survive. And it need not be much, but as *'no man is an island'* (John Donne) we all have some human contact which is required to function across our species.

I would suggest that the work of Rebecca Sax from MIT (Massachusetts Institute of Technology) points to this, where she is published in Nature Neuroscience reporting that social interaction is a basic human need, just like food and water. Similarly, work from the Hoffman Institute show that human interaction is essential for brain development. There is also a plethora of papers on the dangers of lack of human interaction harming mental and physical health (depression, anxiety, obesity, blood pressure). The converse being that connecting with other humans can lower anxiety, help regulate our emotions, lead to higher self-esteem, empathy and even improve our immune system!

In our world so underpinned and led by technology where we can be seemingly so connected, actually we are more socially disconnected than ever before. In order to keep the balance therefore, the HEAD Gardener suggests some level of regular social interaction – even for those for whom it is difficult. We all do things we don't like but know are good for us, and this might be one of yours! But given the evidence about our wellbeing, this small action is as important as having your '5 a day' on the physical health front.

I also want us to look at people and technology from the other end of the telescope, I also believe that we cannot live without technology. We might, in extremis, choose to 'go off grid' or as a friend of mine has done had a No-Facebook-vember so she can remain more attached to the humans around her rather than the rabbit holes that advertising and the web can entice her into, and hours can be lost…

I am not advocating gardening your head without technology or going on some kind of 'crash diet' and disengaging from all technological advancement – I would not be able to either evidence its benefit nor be able to write this book without it! What I am suggesting is using the benefits that technology gives us with a distinct and deliberate purpose to look after our heads, find tools that help us manage the world, and use new research and break throughs to enable us to live happier, healthier, more successful lives. Remember the concept of the HEAD Gardener is for each individual, team and organisation to cultivate success, however you define it.

So as humans, the benefit of technology in all its forms keeps our horizons expanding in many directions. There are offerings of Apps for sleep, diet, meeting people; downloadable pdfs of charts to follow or new regimes; listings of clubs and places or events where other humans will be and of course, dare I say, LinkedIn Monday Matters which I author every Monday to inspire and start your week well and something to discuss with others and the community who follow it!

The third aspect of this curiosity of the balance of technology and people, specifically HEAD gardening, was to find out just how much of our technology could really bridge the distance between the fact and evidence of using a gardening analogy and model for growth with people and the skills needed to truly develop people with the vagaries.

Chat GPT shared the following:

Technology, people and the analogy of the garden can be linked in several ways:

1. *Cultivation and Growth: Like gardeners tend to their plants, technology professionals cultivate and nurture digital systems, software, and hardware to ensure they grow and function optimally.*

2. *Maintenance: Just as a garden requires regular maintenance to thrive, technology experts perform updates, troubleshooting, and maintenance to keep digital systems and software in good working condition.*

3. *Innovation: Gardener's experiment with new plant varieties and techniques to improve their gardens, while technology experts innovate by creating new software, hardware, and solutions to advance the digital landscape.*

4. *Weeding and Security: In both contexts, there's a need to remove unwanted elements. Gardeners weed to keep their garden healthy, and technology professionals address security issues and eliminate malware or vulnerabilities.*

5. *Ecosystem Management: Gardeners strive to create a balanced ecosystem in their gardens. Similarly, technology specialists work on designing and maintaining digital ecosystems that are efficient, secure, and interconnected.*

Overall, the analogy of the garden can be applied to various aspects of technology, emphasizing the care, attention, and planning required to ensure the growth and health of digital systems and innovations.

As you can see, in the blink of an eye, the technology is available to share a fairly congruent and appropriate response. However, the emphasis here is on technological specialists and the work they do rather than the broader spectrum of people and their growth. I wonder if it is the tiny grammatical 'comma' that it has ignored to give the fuller answer? Perhaps that the art and necessity of the human is to ask the right question in the right way for technology to assist with the right answer. Perhaps we both, technology and the human, have some work to do here!

SPIRITUAL AND RELIGOUS GARDENS AND WHAT THEY CAN TEACH US

Many believers in a religious or spiritual force use the structure of nature in gardens, and the concept of the garden itself to provide calm, peace, tranquillity, learning, joy, walking and communing with another source of 'life'. I wanted to share with you 10 versions of gardens that resonate so loudly with the concept of HEAD Gardening that it further excites me of the all the opportunity for all the millions of heads that can connect and grow through these 'gates'.

1. In the Christian Bible, the Garden of Eden is the first garden, where the first humans were given a home by God, and then follows the stories of Adam and Eve eating the apple that they were told not to – the first sin – as this came from the Tree of Knowledge, rather than simply believing in God completely. A further important garden is Gethsemane where Jesus prayed to God before he was crucified, showing the trust he had in Father, and there are over 27 mentions of gardens in the Bible, with the intentions of depicting **peace** and **refreshment** from them.

2. Monastic gardens themselves have also long maintained gardens for **reflection, contemplation**, and **sustenance**. These gardens often include herb gardens for medicinal and culinary use. The Cloisters Museum in New York, a branch of the Metropolitan Museum of Art, features medieval-style gardens that reflect the traditions of Christian monasticism.

3. One of London's oldest & most respected gardens with a unique living collection is the Chelsea Physic Garden, now 350 years old, established in 1673 and home to around 5,000 different edible, useful and medicinal plants. These sorts if gardens have been used for **healing** and for this specific physic garden one of the three key themes of celebration is the role of

gardens and humankind, the role of plants and their benefits for humans. They are cognisant of how this relationship has changed over time and question how humans will benefit from horticulture in the future.

4. For followers of Islam, the concept of a garden is not that of an English Garden which were created for walking in or pleasure but rather specifically for **contemplation** and a place of **restoration**, often planted with aromatic plants and water pools, to appeal to the senses. It is the Islamic Charbagh Gardens that are inspired by the concept of paradise which is promised to believers. The gardens are divided into 4 quadrants by water or walkway – one of the most stunning is that which surrounds The Taj Mahal in India. In this earthly garden it is an analogue for that which;

   Allah has promised to the believing men and the believing women gardens, beneath which rivers flow, to abide in them, and goodly dwellings in gardens of perpetual abode; and best of all is Allah's goodly pleasure; that is the grand achievement.
   – Qur'an 9.72

5. In Japan, Zen gardens, or "karesansui" gardens, are an integral part of Japanese Zen Buddhism. They feature meticulously raked gravel or sand, symbolic rocks, and minimalistic elements. These gardens encourage **meditation** and **mindfulness.**

6. Buddhist temple gardens, like those in the ancient city of Kyoto, Japan, are designed to provide **tranquillity** and space for **meditation.** Kinkaku-ji (the Golden Pavilion) in Kyoto has a beautifully landscaped garden with a reflective pond, symbolic bridges, and carefully chosen plantings.

7. In Sikh places of worship (gurdwaras) these are often beautifully landscaped gardens that reflect the principles of

equality and **community**. The Golden Temple in Amritsar, India, features a large water tank and a serene garden complex that welcomes visitors from all backgrounds.

8. Hindu temple complexes frequently incorporate lush gardens, reflecting the **interconnectedness of nature** and **spirituality**. The Akshardham Temple in Delhi, India, boasts intricately designed gardens featuring water features, sculptures, and manicured landscapes.

9. The Baha'i Faith features meticulously maintained terraced gardens, notably the Bahá'í Gardens in Haifa, Israel, and on Mount Carmel. These gardens symbolize the faith's principles of **unity** and **harmony**.

10. Some Native American tribes create medicine wheel gardens, which are circular stone arrangements that hold spiritual significance. The gardens are used for **ceremonies, meditation**, and **healing** rituals.

If we look at the text in bold across these 10 different religious and spiritual gardens, we can see that they serve as a physical embodiment of the specific spiritual beliefs and traditions. They support the believer, or offer the visitors, a space for reflection, connection with the divine, and a deeper understanding of their respective faiths. They speak to the diversity and cultural significance of religious gardens around the world and also how much our human selves and the heads we use to guide us are nurtured and grown through gardens themselves.

A garden is your own idea of heaven.

Being The HEAD Gardener I have the honour to help you shape that idea, and then be there to support you cultivate that heaven on earth.

- 6 -

USEFUL CHECKLISTS

The 10 Mistakes HEAD Gardeners Make

1. Throwing out plants without seeing a full cycle or what they could do somewhere else!

2. Putting too much in one 'border' (or asking too much of one department) makes it crowded and confused, with plants fighting for light and food rather than focussing on growth.

3. Letting one flower dominate which looks good initially but detracts from the other equally promising plants who haven't been given the attention or the opportunity to show off.

4. Leaving plants to 'get on with it' without any direction or support. Doing so will have them wither away, strangle others or quietly go somewhere else! Not a recipe for harmony or success.

5. Imagining that once potted-on a plant never needs anything else, or if it does it will ask.

6. Telling a plant to grow, and that this will be sufficient to make it so.

7. Believing you are always going to get your choice of action right.

8. Leaving it to lady luck rather than hard graft to get the outcome you want.

9. Working against nature.

10. Giving up.

The 10 Top Tips for Cultivating Success

1. Have the patience to see through your vision even if results are not immediately obvious. If you have done the work, it will come good.

2. Be clear what you do and don't want – and make it known (remember a weed is only a plant in the 'wrong' place).

3. Every plant can grow a little taller and brighter with a bit of help and support.

4. Look ahead at the 'weather' forecast before you take action, and look outside your 'window' to see what the weather is really doing now!

5. It's possible to over-garden over-water and over-worry. Stand back and let nature play a hand, it does know best.

6. Ignore people who tell you that you can't do something. They have no idea how good you are and if you want it badly enough, one day you will succeed.

7. Focus on outcome not output – how you change the world not how many 'whatevers' you produce.

8. Some people will distance themselves from you when you trip up yet want part of the success when that comes to. Look out for them and work out just how generous you want to be.

9. Saying what you think is rarely a bad thing, not saying it usually is.

10. Trust yourself and your God/instinct, and your HEAD garden will thrive!

My Checklist

You can complete this exercise (opposite) 4 times in a year. Start with whichever season you are in within the annual calendar, and decide:

> (1) one thing you will start doing

> (2) one thing you will stop doing and

> (3) one thing you will continue to do in order to garden your head. That way, you can begin the journey to cultivate the success you are seeking.

Come back to this every quarter and check in with yourself to see:

> (1) how you are doing

> (2) what you are doing, and

> (3) what you need to do next.

	Start	Stop	Keep doing
SPRING			
SUMMER			
AUTUMN			
WINTER			

EPILOGUE

In Part 3 it is the four short essays that have been deliberately structured into 4 quadrants, like the Chabagh, as it is these 4 aspects that are all held in our heads at the same time, affect our choices and how we grow and help others in the garden that we inhabit.

For each one of us, and those we lead, interact with, support, ask of and care for – professionally or personally – are the human embodiment of the garden and how it survives and thrives, or doesn't. The garden is a living body, and we should treat it like one and ours like we tend a garden.

We are the ones who leave a legacy for the next generation and create the gardens that they can tend and prosper through, and as 'real' gardeners know, we garden for tomorrow, because the true benefit and fruits of our labours comes many years after we are gone, and shape the pleasure, sustenance and optimism for the future we will not see.

ABOUT THE AUTHOR

Caroline has spent her career helping people to improve their lives to be happy and successful. From a career beginning in nursing, through to a global consultancy she has learnt where people grow and thrive and how often their growth is stunted by lack of care or planning or simply being overwhelmed by process and bureaucracy.

After working in the public and private sector Caroline decided it was time to go back to her roots, go back to investing in what really matters and makes the difference, and that is the growth of people.

This book is sector agnostic, useful in all aspects of business development and architecture as well as being applicable to individuals, teams and change in organisations.

She is NOT a gardener but uses the principles and concept of gardens and gardening to create results. As the speed of technology and innovation in our world continues to rise, she believes that the growth of the human self, and in teams, needs ever more attention to use it most effectively, and to help all people to become their best selves. Her overriding purpose is to leave the world in a better place than when she found it, so she has become The HEAD Gardener.